PENGUIN BOOKS

DISPATCHES FROM THE POVERTY LINE

Pat Capponi is the author of the critically acclaimed memoir *Upstairs in the Crazy House*. She is also one of Canada's leading mental health care advocates. As well as participating in numerous government hearings, task forces and inquests, Pat is a founding board member of the Gerstein Centre in Toronto.

D1516121

dispatches
from the
poverty line

pat
capponi

Penguin Books

PENGUIN BOOKS
Published by the Penguin Group
Penguin Books Canada Ltd, 10 Alcorn Avenue, Toronto, Ontario,
Canada M4V 3B2
Penguin Books Ltd, 27 Wrights Lane, London W8 5TZ, England
Viking Penguin, a division of Penguin Books USA Inc., 375 Hudson Street, New York,
New York 10014, U.S.A.
Penguin Books Australia Ltd, Ringwood, Victoria, Australia
Penguin Books (NZ) Ltd, cnr Rosedale and Airborne Roads, Albany,
Auckland 1310, New Zealand

Penguin Books Ltd, Registered Offices: Harmondsworth,
Middlesex, England

First published 1997

3 5 7 9 10 8 6 4

Printed and bound in Canada on acid free paper ∞

Canadian Cataloguing in Publication Data

Capponi, Pat, 1949–
Dispatches from the poverty line

ISBN 0-14-026233-4

I. Poor — Canada. 2. Canada — Social policy. 3. Social security — Canada.
I. Title

HC120.P6C36 1997   362.5'0971   C96-931471-X

Visit Penguin Canada's web site at **www.penguin.ca**

Excerpts from the author's open letter to Mike Harris, first published in
NOW magazine (February 22–28, 1996), reproduced by permission.

Paul Quinn
Nora McCabe
Reva Gerstein
Dianne Capponi
Cynthia Good
Joey Slinger
June Callwood
John Russell
Ernest Hirschbach
Meg Masters
Scott Sellers
Bev Slopen
Sandra Capponi
Catherine Marjoribanks
Marc Lafontaine
Bob Buckingham
Laurie Hall
Julia Capponi
family past and present;
those who came forward;
the crew at A-way Express;
and the good folks at
NOW magazine

thank you

preface

*At the annual general meeting of the [Psychiatric] Consumer/
Survivor Information Centre, where I am scheduled to speak, I am
gently chastised by a man who must hold his torn pants together with
safety pins, whose arthritis has settled deep into his hips, whose poverty is palpable: "I was very concerned about you, you know, after I read
that article you wrote in NOW magazine."*

My current story is not a typical one, not the classic "person
living in poverty" saga. I have lived that way, in the past, when
I was a young person escaping a history of abuse, trying to
start anew, but finding myself anonymous and isolated and
hungry and lost. Those were black days, even though there was
still a social safety net of sorts.

Now I am neither isolated nor anonymous. I am given
frequent day parole from poverty: I have friends who are rather
insistent about helping out. And I have the remains of a successful career that still provides the occasional injection of
cash. Above all, I have options and choices, even if, for a series
of complex reasons, I have often chosen not to exercise them.
But the despair of the last years of unemployment and hunger
reminds me again and again that most people living in poverty
only know others in the same circumstances, people who

cannot even provide temporary relief from their empty pockets and empty shelves. For most, poverty is a closed circle.

And I have something else that the poor generally do without: I have people who value me and words to describe what I and others are going through. Because I can bring you dispatches from the poverty line, I will. Because I continue to live in two very different worlds, I continue to search for ways to bring them together.

dispatches
from the
poverty line

isaster preparedness.

It's not the kind of training that well-meaning occupational therapists tried to instil in me during and after each hospitalization on psychiatric wards.

"What do you plan to eat for supper during the coming week? Let's make up a menu, and then we'll see what you need to shop for and prepare."

"What will you do to keep busy at home on the weekends? Wouldn't it do you good to arrange to meet someone, go for a walk or have lunch at a restaurant?"

I endured the relentlessly cheerful chatter, learned to nod at the appropriate points, even made things up if I had to, so that my notation for the day would read: "Patient co-operative and

3

making plans for return home, seems to be looking forward to her day of discharge."

This is a different kind of planning, of preparation. I have counted and recounted my remaining funds.

It's September now, and I have enough to cover the rent until January 1, 1996. I'll have two hundred dollars left over, if I let the phone go. I have no other income to count on, no job prospects. I'm trying to shake off the feeling that I've just had quick-hardening cement poured over my head. Or that the four-point restraining cuffs have just been attached to my wrists and ankles, and the attendant has left the room.

I'm rigid with tension, sitting knees to chest on my futon, my back against the wall, staring out at the schoolyard, which will soon be alive with great gusts of shouts and laughter as the kids take their recess—as if the leaves aren't falling from the trees, as if the ground will never harden, as if snow and ice and frigid temperatures aren't ready to pounce.

It's not as though I'd ever expected to stay safe and comfortable the rest of my life. I've never been able to buy into the majority view that one can impose personal and financial order on chaos, careful planning on happenstance, a cleared and picket-fenced path through the jungle that surrounds us. I've never lost sight of the jungle, the ominous glow of eyes in the dark, the screams of the devoured and the full-throated howls of the temporarily victorious. There are things about life, about people, it is better to never know; but once you know, it becomes impossible to believe in the shared illusions of safety and entitlement and reason.

I've lived in this room in Toronto's Annex neighbourhood for five years, the longest I've lived anywhere since coming to

Toronto in 1978. It is small, not well maintained. There is a full bathroom and an alcove that serves as a kitchenette, housing a bar-sized fridge and a toaster oven.

My rent, $475, is an amount I believed I would always be able to meet, whether or not I was gainfully employed. My version of security. I've tried to hoard items such as canned goods and cleaning supplies, but there isn't a great deal of storage space, unless I want to pile goods against the four walls as a bulwark against reality. To quell my rising sense of panic, I've decided to take stock of what's in the cupboards, what stands between me and disaster.

> 3 tins of corn
>
> 6 tins of Irish stew
>
> 3 tins of salmon
>
> 2 tins of corn beef hash
>
> 1 jar ($\frac{3}{4}$ full) of instant coffee
>
> 2 tins of ground coffee
>
> 1 large bottle of coffee creamer
>
> 2 boxes of artificial sweetener
>
> 1 large jar of peanut butter
>
> 2 mason jars of birdseed for my canary, Ricco
>
> 2 tins of whole potatoes
>
> 2 tins of smoked oysters
>
> 2 tins of chili
>
> 1 jar of salsa
>
> 1 (almost full) jar of mayonnaise
>
> 1 jar of mustard

$\frac{1}{2}$ bottle of vinegar

6 packs of cigarettes

16 rolls of (one-ply) toilet paper

4 rolls of paper towels

1 large bottle of aspirin

6 as yet unread books

4 bars of face soap

4 new razor blades

1 half-full tin of spray deodorant

1 box of tampons

1 tube of toothpaste

1 unused notebook

8 shirts still in their dry cleaner bags

3 clean pairs of jeans

I made another list—of the things stacked against me.

A phone bill I won't be able to pay

A cable bill

A hole in the sole of my cowboy boots

No migraine pills

No emergency back-up eyeglasses

No emergency transit tickets

No winter scarf

No winter boots

I feel like an inept survivalist, victim of his own inadequate planning in the face of expected disaster. I immediately determine to put myself on a rationing regime. Until something comes up. I try to kid myself that something will come up.

It's not like I haven't been down-and-out poor before. Not like I'm a stranger to hunger.

The first thing I have to do is get my stomach used to less. The worst thing about hunger is the headaches it gives you, which for me always threaten to escalate into migraines, and I can't afford $100 for six pills, the cost of the miracle medication.

Drinking lots of water can fool the stomach into believing it's had more than it really has had. Step one.

Step two. Ration cigarettes. Put an open pack in the fridge instead of right where I can see and reach for them without thinking.

Step three. Go out immediately and convert the bulk of my remaining cash into money orders made out to my landlord: don't trust that common sense will prevail over immediate need. I've had to make the choice a number of times in my life, whether to eat or keep a roof over my head.

We are told by the media that most Americans are two or three paycheques from the street. I've already beaten those odds. Over four months now with no income, and I can still pay for three months of walls and a door with a lock on it.

And something will come up.

Won't it?

—·—·—

I don't spend a lot of time mourning my personal circumstances, my personal loss. There is so much to grieve for.

So much destruction.

Everyone wants to be seen as a victim, these days. I've never understood the attraction. Real victims never understand that they are victims.

In the first two decades of my life, which of course included the formative years, no one ever broke through the sanctity of our family to tell the children: You do know you are the victims here, right?

In fact, we grew up feeling just the opposite, and had that confirmed at school, and in other contacts with the world outside our front door. There would have been no violent beatings if we hadn't brought them on ourselves: whether five months old or seventeen years, we were responsible, we deserved what we got. We weren't good enough, quiet enough, clean enough, smart enough, invisible enough to make our presence tolerable.

When I hear Mrs. Clinton say "It takes a village to raise a child," and Bob Dole counter with "It takes a family," I can't help thinking that neither concept did much for us. Every family in our community that heard the screams or saw the results kept their own counsel. And teachers who were left to deal with the symptoms of the abused children reacted only to the symptoms and not the cause, confirming that we were our own victimizers.

In eighteen years, I don't remember a day that didn't begin and end in fear. It would have taken a much stronger person than me not to internalize all that blame and guilt for being alive, and a much wiser individual to understand exactly how those feelings would affect my later life.

It wasn't surprising, then, that I spent most of my time wishing I didn't exist, feeling I had to constantly justify being alive. Nobody takes the time to tell children from abusive homes the right way to ask for help, and you're very aware that you're not supposed to ask at all. And because you don't feel as though you're worth much, you can't really trust that asking will bring anything but confirmation of your "badness."

I spent a good ten years, in between college, university and work, flailing about, looking to feel better about who I was, and where I belonged, looking to be fixed. I seem to have looked in all the wrong places, in all the wrong ways. Seven hospitalizations later, in 1978, I found myself in a psychiatric boarding home in west-end Toronto, with seventy other chronic patients, truly at the end of the line.

It was a place where I experienced a long, drawn-out epiphany about mental illness, and about therapeutic intervention and its limitations. I examined what I was looking for, and how I could come to terms with my own suicidal feelings and their expression. I stopped looking for outside intervention and decided to fence in my self-destructive behaviour with a set of rules that served me well for the next two decades of my life.

The first rule was: No more suicide "attempts." Attempts would only land me in hospital. Hospital sends me to the madhouse. The next time I tried to kill myself would have to be the last time, rescue and intervention and change-of-mind proof.

In the past, I had tried all the traditional and non-traditional ways. Set myself alight, overdosed on prescription and street

drugs, cut veins and swallowed a variety of lethal items—
straight pins, pieces of razor blades and glass. I'd experimented
with slashing, cigarette burns, heating the blade of a knife and
pressing the red-hot metal on my flesh. And wound up on
wards and in treatments that did nothing to alleviate the pain
that drove me towards self-destruction.

No rescue, no cure. Those four words became my private
mantra.

I made my pact with the world. I will live as long as I'm
doing things that make a difference, because that's the only
activity I've found that makes me feel better about who I am.
When I'm overwhelmed by suicidal impulses, I will wait them
out, in private, out of sight of professionals and friends. If I lose
out to them, those seductive urges, so be it. It's not really a loss
at all, but a release. If I emerge alive, that's okay too. But nothing in between.

I first had suicidal wishes when I was ten, and have never
lost them. They've become an emergency escape plan, comforting, always there, always with me, like a promise, like the
light at the end of a long, frightening tunnel. I had no wish
to escape them any more, just to control them until I really
needed them.

Within this framework, I found I could be productive, even
happy.

I learned to like who I was. I got through every bad time, by
myself, and found myself getting stronger and stronger.

I went from the boarding home to a job as a community
worker at a drop-in called PARC, the Parkdale Activity and
Recreation Centre, whose clients were discharged chronic
psychiatric patients living in rooming and boarding homes in

the Parkdale area of Toronto. I came to feel a sense of mission, a strong sense of purpose: this is why I'd been through all I'd been through, in order to achieve the sensitivity and education to help better the living conditions of people much like me. Fair enough.

Then followed six years of front-line work, of feeling all the misery and futility around me, of small victories and so many lonely deaths and suicides. I was tired and filled with dread: what if those six years, and all the years that went before, were only the necessary training for yet another mission—a mission more desperate and dreadful? I was exhausted, physically and emotionally; I prayed for a terminal illness the way some kids pray for cars and credit cards. But then, in 1995, I contracted with the Ontario government to do leadership facilitation with members of my population around the province. I would be enabling "chronic psychiatric patients" to participate in the planning, management and delivery of mental health services and fostering the development of regional psychiatric survivor groups. I had a hefty salary, a good budget, an assistant and, even better, I was based at the Gerstein Centre. The Gerstein Centre is a non-medical facility for those in psycho-social crisis, named for Reva Gerstein, who is almost an institution herself in the psychiatric survivor community. I first met Reva when she was appointed to the Mayor's Action Task Force on Discharged Psychiatric Patients, and I was lucky enough to have been part of the founding of the Centre. Paul Quinn, my co-worker and friend from PARC, was also working there as co-director.

It felt like a form of renewal, being able to enlist others into the struggle, working with them to find ways and means of representing our population at government, institution and agency tables. Watching others learn what I had about how much better you feel when you fight back.

Four years had passed swiftly. I had written and published a book about my boarding home and those in it, *Upstairs in the Crazy House*, sold the movie rights, won awards for advocacy, gone to other provinces to give speeches, hold workshops and teach leadership development. I was happy. How could I not be? What more can a person ask than the right to contribute? But I never lost my readiness to leave.

I would stop every now and then, take a moment to ask myself, usually at the best times: "Is this enough to make you change your mind?" It was oddly comforting that the answer always came back "No."

I went through the silent, private struggles when they arose, always able to point out to myself that I was still making a difference, so I couldn't die now. It would be abandonment.

Then I was appointed to the Ontario Advocacy Commission, a body that was to create a system of advocates and rights advisers throughout different regions and institutions in the province. The communities we would serve would include the elderly, disabled, mentally handicapped and those in psychiatric hospitals. We had five months of existence, until the provincial election, and the new premier, and the clawback, and the freeze and the dismantling.

I confess, underneath all the disappointment and anger and bewilderment, I felt a certain relief at no longer having a platform, or the means to struggle on.

I was out of a job, but I couldn't go on welfare, couldn't imagine putting my hand out in this climate. I was no longer eligible for unemployment insurance, which I had relied on when my leadership facilitation contract ended. I watched and listened to Mike Harris's first act as premier, cutting welfare rates. I felt his contempt and the weight of his judgments. I saw something too familiar in his face. I would keep my dignity, despite the cost.

And work? Part of my survival had always involved not putting myself into situations that would exacerbate my negative feelings about myself and my capabilities. I remember a surprised worker interpreting the results of vocational and psychological testing for me.

"It seems you refuse to try anything you're not good at."

As much as I'd accepted the necessity of the kind of upbringing I'd endured, parts of it could still bushwhack me, if I wasn't careful.

I might have been able to flip burgers, if only I could have flipped them competently. But I freeze up when trying to learn new things in that kind of work situation, as though my body and mind are in some kind of time warp, anticipating the violence of fists or accusations of stupidity. I have tried, in the past, factory work, collections, dish-washing, cleaning, waitressing—I was pathetic. And I *felt* pathetic, which usually contributed to yet another hospital admission.

I've never believed my life was worth living at any cost.

There seemed to be nothing left for me to do. I wouldn't even be able to keep my room in a couple of months. I was finished. I was done. Wasn't I?

I'm a religious person, and I wanted some kind of endorsement from God for the conclusion I'd reached. It seemed to come days later, when I started keeping a journal about living on the brink of homelessness. My last advocacy act, that's how I thought about it, and I was grateful that my solitary death would have some meaning beyond simple defeat.

Show the government, in graphic terms, what their policies do to people. I wouldn't be enduring simply for the sake of enduring—something I've never understood. There would be a purpose, even meaning.

In late November I began my daily journal in letter form. I had told my friend and publisher Cynthia Good that just listening to Harris or his spokespeople was driving me nuts. The anger I was feeling was overwhelming—more so because there was no place, no position from which to speak, to fight back.

She told me to write it down.

I thought about that. But to what purpose? More importantly, to what effect?

My own situation was bleak and threatening, but I'd been there before and probably would be again. (My life is so full of ups and downs I'm thinking of putting in an escalator.) It was just the nature of my uneasy relationship with the world, insignificant in the face of the greater harm being done on a daily basis to those least able to survive it.

It was yet another Harris statement that forced my hand. He was acknowledging that some people might be hurting over Christmas, and he regretted that, but he was sure people understood it as necessary.

His standing at the polls was high, higher than the night he won the election. I was rereading Tolkien's *Lord of the Rings*, and real life seemed to be playing it out, as vividly bent on evil as Tolkien's worst villains.

So I booted up my computer, taking it as a good omen that

it did not beep at me alarmingly, and started:

"Dear Mike Harris ..."

Over the next days and weeks, I explained my state of mind and state of life, emphasizing the precarious nature of a life swallowed whole by poverty. In the original journal, I was outlining each of the thirty-one days I had to go before a rent day came that I was unable to meet.

It was a time during which I grew occasionally nostalgic about the times when I'd actually had the choice of eating *and* paying rent.

As one long day followed another, my writing grew more intense, more focused. It was all I was doing. Which begged the question: what do I do with it now?

-.-.-

It was late on a Friday evening in February. No one in the know used my apartment buzzer when the weather dipped below zero, as it tended to freeze into muteness, so the rapping on the window didn't so much alarm as alert me that a visitor was calling.

I went out the door to my room and let my good friend Nora McCabe in, along with a bluster of cold air and whirl of snowflakes and stomping of boots. It wasn't much warmer in my room; Ricco, my canary, had already gone to sleep bitching under his breath, after first stretching one arthritic leg, then the other.

A quick hug, and then: "Good news, we've got good news!" Toronto's weekly *NOW* magazine wanted to run my journal entries as an article. I had asked Nora's husband Joey, a columnist for the *Toronto Star,* to make the deal for me. "C'mon, put your hat and coat on, we'll go celebrate at Dooney's. Joey's waiting in the car."

I was almost weak-kneed with relief, with validation, that the last four months had a purpose, however small, a reason, however obscure. A quick and silent prayer of thanks, offered to the ceiling, as I shrugged into my jacket.

Nora continued: "They had no number they could reach you at, but I told them you'd call first thing Monday morning. Pat, you've got to let us reconnect your phone!"

An on-again, off-again argument I paid no attention to as I slipped on my running shoes and followed her happily back out into the snow.

t first, it felt like an invasion. As though outside forces had gathered in secret on our borders and in one fell swoop taken over the streets and government. It was evocative, for me, of the federal soldiers taking up positions in Montreal during the October crisis, occupying—or so it felt—our province.

But this was no army of strangers. These were friends, neighbours, co-workers; this was legitimate, this was democracy.

For four months, I, and others like me, had watched in stunned silence as Ontario declared war on the poor, the disabled, the elderly, the different; declared itself open for business for the taxpayer, for the banks. I listened to the applause for the premier and watched his approval ratings soar.

It wasn't just Ontario, of course; North America was in the

grip of an emotional deep freeze—people wanted affirmation that they were being used and abused by the underclasses, and politicians gave them what they wanted. They cut food stamps, cut school lunch programs, cut moneys available to single mothers, brought in "workfare."

I heard myself and others like me defined as "special interest groups," forced to occupy the role previously held by business, by paid lobbyists. I heard the premier's firm resolve to stand against us. I stayed home. Watched Newsworld and CNN and tried to understand what was happening. Where had all the people gone?

Dear Mike Harris,

Since your election, I can't believe any more. There was a time when faces like yours, contemptuous and sure, took away everything that made life livable. I will not go to welfare, hold out my hand and say, please, sir. There is a dignity in my hunger, even in my fear. I believe it is better to be who I am, even now, than to be you.

It bothers me that I can't be awake without using up something. A cigarette, a bagel, something. I'm waking up at different times during the night, sometimes incapable of getting back to sleep, so that the hours of want stretch from 4:00 a.m. to midnight. I'm immersed in need; there's no room for anything else. I don't allow myself to think, not about tomorrow, or next week—that will produce panic, and it takes a great deal of energy to clamp down and simply endure.

I was relieved when the phone was cut off in November. I couldn't trust to my own resolve, my rapidly diminishing strength, to overcome impulses to reach out for help. When I am down, due to circumstance or depression, I require time and privacy and inviolate space. It is difficult enough to emerge unscathed from bad times without having to put on an exhausting front so people won't worry, don't interfere. In order to keep myself going, these are the kinds of accommodations I must make. You won't find them in any disability handbook.

It's easier now that winter has closed in, causing me to feel cut off from the world out there—I don't go out, nothing comes in. It's safety, of a sort.

The worst days are when I can't write, when there's nothing to show for the long hours of silent misery. It's hard, though, to chronicle a life that's reduced to such extremes. For the last week, I've lived on two bagels a day, and seemingly gallons of water.

I watch the news, listen to government pronouncements. As bad, as difficult as it is for me, I am very aware of how much I have compared with most of the poor. I still have walls around me, and a door that locks, though these things feel much less substantial now that they are threatened. I have words to describe what I feel. I have some perspective on government and bureaucracy. I have friends, though right now friendship and caring are fearful things.

I'm very determined to stay the course, to accept whatever happens to me, as determined as Mike Harris. And I know others would find my decision appalling. I'm used to hiding what I feel and think, in order to stay safe. My friends have become used to abiding by the rules I draw around my life, and my increasingly reclusive nature.

Sometimes the edges of my life seem trimmed with psychosis, glimpsed but not possessed. I grew up distorted by an "angry white male with a bad haircut" whose name was Mike, who resented, even hated, those dependent on him. I learned I was the cause of every evil, imagined or real. The need to be corrected played out in blows.

In a neighbourhood of the willfully deaf and blind 46 years later, having finally learned to stand up and feel counted, I am again diminished, silenced and blamed by an angry white man with a bad haircut named Mike who speaks of the need for correction. Full circle.

It's about a month since my open letter appeared in *NOW* magazine (picture and all, I remember uncomfortably, scrunching down a little more in my seat). The unexpected bonus was that my editor at Penguin Books saw the piece and approached me to write this book. It would be based on journal entries, as well as a series of interviews I wanted to do. With borrowed resources, I faxed a flyer to various agencies and services in Metro, asking those affected by Harris's cuts to come forward and tell their stories. Those that were resonant to me I followed up on, and the book emerged.

Just a few hours ago, I walked over to see my agent, Bev Slopen, and together we waded through the technical language of the contract with Penguin. Home continues to be a rather bleak place for me: my fridge is still empty, my shelves and wallet still bare. I wasn't overly anxious to return to those four walls, so when Bev told me a friend of hers had an extra ticket to a benefit that night organized by PEN, an international organization of writers that supports writers in crisis and advocates freedom of expression, I agreed to go.

She is very pleased for me, for this new contract to produce *Dispatches from the Poverty Line* for Penguin. Last week she sent her assistant to my place with two bottles of wine, a carton of cigarettes and a coupon for a free pizza. She has insisted on paying to reconnect my phone, throwing in enough to cover several months of service. In other words, not your typical literary agent. When we finished the tedious reading and initialling and signing and dating of the contract, she turned into a homemaker and scared up supper for us, mentioning as an aside that we'd be meeting a friend of hers at a book launch. The party is for Hugh Segal's new book—Segal is a former adviser to Brian Mulroney—and it's taking place at the Park Plaza on Bloor Street. We'd meet her friend there and travel to the PEN benefit together.

Which is why I'm now at the Park Plaza, desperately smoking, while Bev networks.

You couldn't pack much more well-being into a room if you tried. I'm surrounded by healthy, high-income men and women: the remnants of Ontario's old Conservative Party.

In my jeans and black leather jacket and hat, I'm feeling extremely conspicuous: the troll under the bridge, the fly in the ointment, the worm in the apple. Nobody has come up to me (which I'd half expected) and demanded to see my invitation—

no one's called security to have me escorted out. So far.

There's a tiny group of smokers gathered around the table I'm seated at—it's almost the only one in the room—and I haven't budged since I followed my agent in.

Two men appear, dragging cigarette packs from their suit jackets. They make a valiant attempt to strike up a conversation, but to me it sounds like: *What are you doing here?*

Somewhat defensively, I say: "I'm here with my agent."

Because I have an agent and long, straight hair and wear a hat, they wonder if I'm with a band.

"No, I'm writing a book."

"What about?"

"Poverty."

They laugh, a good, honest laugh that emphasizes irony, and I laugh with them.

"Boy, are you in the wrong place." One of them grins.

That feels better, though they're pretty quick to leave. The speeches are starting anyway.

I watch an ageing Bill Davis make his way to the podium, and I can't help remembering back to when he was premier, and I was in the boarding house with all the other crazy people. De-institutionalization of chronic psychiatric patients started under his watch, and I remember trying to understand why they couldn't see the consequences of their ill-thought-out policies. I started my advocacy career in that house, and went on to fight during the Liberal and NDP eras.

As bad as it was in the beginning, and it was very bad, there was—for me at least—hope that things would get better. That once we exposed our living conditions, our good neighbours and our elected representatives would be moved to act. I worked for the next two decades to make improvements in the system that oppressed us.

I stare at him now, and at the audience, and wonder how everything fell apart, wonder how you reach out to those whose life experience is so different, whose palpable sense of entitlement and privilege is so blinding they will not see.

I was ready to go a half-hour ago, but now I'm really ready. Thankfully, so are Bev and her friend. We make our way to the elevator. I feel as though I've been claimed (along with a coat), and move more easily through the stalled people. A personable young man accompanies us; he also is heading to the PEN event, and offers us a lift, which we take. It seems to be a night of continuing irony: he is the publisher of the *Financial Post*. I shake my head and bite the insides of my cheeks, wishing that just one of these people could look and act like what they do —like Mr. Burns from "The Simpsons," for instance. Someone you could love to hate. But the world ain't that simple.

Or that easy.

I can't follow the conversation too well; it's not deliberately exclusive, it just generously assumes too much insider knowledge, so I tune out and begin to wonder if I'll feel more at home at this event than at the other.

When I was much younger, during those rare times when I could envision a future, I told myself that I wanted to be something that would allow me to move through the different classes and professions unobstructed. I've clearly achieved that, to an astonishing degree. The downside, of course, is that I have no sense of belonging anywhere, though my loyalties are clearly with "the have-nots."

I tell myself, I am a published writer. And a published writer with another contract with a major house ... who's left her cigarettes at the Park Plaza! I curse myself briefly, silently. I'll be walking home, having just about enough in my pocket for another pack if I don't have to pay subway or bus fare.

Being a gentleman, our friend drops us off in front of the theatre before he looks for a parking space, and I trail the two ladies to the inside box office, where we retrieve my ticket.

I excuse myself and go looking for cigarettes, but this isn't a neighbourhood that grows variety stores on every corner, so I end up in a hotel tuck shop, paying extortionate rates for a brand that's not mine. Now there is only loose change clattering in the pocket of my jeans, but a lit cigarette relieves some of the tension as I approach once again the large crowd mingling in front of the theatre. I don't want to go in, it's nice out here. The rain stopped a while ago, and the streets smell clean and damp.

I try a pep talk again as I light another: You are a writer, you know. Check your wallet, you even have an expired Writers' Union card.

Ah well. I toss away the butt, take a deep breath and plunge inside. Almost immediately I spot June Callwood, author and social activist and friend, and her husband, Trent Frayne. June came up with the title of my first book and wrote a glowing introduction. Her irreverence and obvious pleasure in seeing me help me to relax in the opulent theatre. Judith Thompson, a playwright who is working on the screenplay for the film version of my book, calls out to me from a table where she sits flogging PEN merchandise.

It's an odd way to embark on a new task, but it probably beats being smashed over the head with a champagne bottle.

Here I am surrounded by writers and the intelligentsia, listening to a tribute to the recently martyred Nigerian author Ken Saro-Wiwa, having just come from a gathering of those who define power. Then, finally, a break. There is a silent auction. One is supposed to circulate and write out bids. This of course is beyond my means, in spite of the exhortation to "Spend!"

I hear someone shout "Smoke!" Outside in the cavernous lobby, everything is shut down; it's like being trapped in a huge elevator. I've spent so much time in terrible solitude that I'm overwhelmed. Nobody is moving, everybody is shoulder to cramped shoulder. It's unbelievable, I'm stricken, unable to catch a breath. All I can see is people. After a few panicky moments, I do detect some movement—painful, slow, sluggish, but still ...

I'm positioned behind a guy, which is good, because I'm no better at making headway than I am at networking. I follow in his miserly wake. Outside! A little shakily, I pull a cigarette from my pack and light up, coughing with relief. I don't want to go back in.

I try, handicapped with a terrible sense of direction, to figure out where I am and the best way to get home. If I do decide to take off.

"Want a lift home?"

I whirl around, and there's Nora McCabe and Joey Slinger, mercifully grinning at me. I grin back: "Oh, yeah. But what's the etiquette when you have a free ticket? Is it rude?"

Nora says, "Just tell them you were kidnapped by Slinger."

Deal.

All this, and a ride home with my favourite couple, too. It's a beautiful night, and I babble for a bit about the fog or mist or whatever is gathered around the streetlights. And the Segal launch, in all its strangeness.

Not till I lock my door behind me do I remember the circumstances in which I'm living. I don't remember so much as have them crashing down on me: tomorrow's hunger, yet another rent day looming. To hell with it, I determine, for tonight at least let's pretend. It was a good night, and it might be a better morning.

ast week, in yet another attempt to establish some modicum of control over my life, I counted my pennies and went out and purchased mouse traps.

When I discovered the first bold intruder, I felt as outraged as the Italian housewives who harassed the homeless guy right off their street, slapping at him, cursing him, moving him along. He was worse than the dripping tap, worse than the hunger headache, a sign of the times, of my impotence in the face of adversity.

I tried to get him to misstep his way into a wastebasket. I layered the bottom with canary seeds (which is the only reason he's here in the first place, since mice have an unusual attraction to canary seed) and placed a thin sheet of paper on top, like an African big-game hunter digging and

31

camouflaging a pit.

Of course, this didn't work, and before I knew it my one aggravating mouse had become two, two who liked to chase each other around the narrow confines of my room. For days neither the rodents nor I quite grasped the concept of the mouse trap—they feasted and belched their way through the blobs of peanut butter with nary a snap.

I'm someone who let the holes in her ears grow over due to a squeamish inability to put in my own earrings: my knees would turn to water when I tried. I hate mouse traps because if they fulfil their purpose, you're left having to ... throw away the results.

Every murderer is faced with the same question: what to do with the corpse? It took all my emotional reserves to rid myself of the first body, two days ago. Then yesterday, I heard a scuttle, or a flop, and I couldn't bear it. My room is far too small to share with a corpse.

I spent two-thirds of the day sitting on my stoop, hoping for a kindly macho passerby. It's summer—too hot to leave an unburied body lying around. One friend gave me a fairly brilliant suggestion, though: take off your glasses first, then throw some newspaper over the blurry area. I was working my way up to that—by hyperventilating as I sat outside.

I share the street with a women's shelter and a teenagers' group home, and like an answered prayer I spied a staff member from the Gerstein Centre walking along with another staff member from the shelter on her way to put in a moonlighting shift. I walked out to meet them before they went inside.

"Darna, are you squeamish?"

I explained my problem, and being true crisis workers they

came back to my room with me, prepared to get rid of the evidence. Both traps were empty. I hadn't gotten up the nerve to actually check that there was a body, you see, it was just the sounds that filled in the blanks.

They laughed, but not too much, conscious of my embarrassment; I was feeling like one of those poor souls who regularly confess to murders they hear about on the news.

Today, I do have a victim. I edged up to the trap, which I'd hidden behind a box, scrunched up my eyes, spotted the tail and broke into a sweat.

Motivated by a different kind of desperation, I have decided to try and sell off some of my books and clothing in a garage sale, without the garage. On the tiny scrub of lawn outside my building, I have neatly laid out hardcover and pocket books, my Walkman, a suede jacket and a suit jacket I've worn only three times. To me, selling books is akin to selling children, but I have nothing else of real monetary value that I can pawn or flog. I am out of coffee filters, and though I am aware that you can substitute paper towels, I'm also out of those. I have half a pack of cigarettes, and I am so heartily sick of day-old bagels that hunger is almost preferable.

I started around eleven, now it's two, and I'm composing a bad poem in my head about spilling your life across a lawn and no one seeing in it anything worth having. I have two dollars more than I started out with, a mouldering corpse looming in a corner of my room and no takers for my life.

A young man rides up on his bike to peruse the titles and tries on the suit jacket, tries out the Walkman, while telling me he's spent all his cash for the day.

He sits beside me on the stoop, and I learn he is a French Canadian from Montreal, and we swap stories about our home town. He worked for the government in Ontario and was laid off in 1995. He tries to believe it was the best thing that ever happened to him.

We cut a deal for the jacket and the Walkman: he puts five dollars down and will pay off the remainder over the next couple of weeks, like a layaway plan.

We're still chatting when Nora pulls up in her car, surprising me because no one just drops by without phoning, since I'm unlikely to answer the bell. I find myself flushed with embarrassment at this visible display of need, and to cover myself I say:

"Sorry, you must have called but I've been outside all day ..."

"No, I was just on my way to Andrea's and I thought you might want to come for coffee later."

I introduce her to my new friend and promise to be here when she swings by again after visiting her daughter in about an hour.

No takers for the next sixty minutes, so when Nora reappears I'm quite ready to pack it in. She helps me bring the piles of stuff back inside and makes use of my bathroom while I tidy up the last of the sale items. When I come back into the room, I persuade her to check the other trap, which is thankfully empty. She volunteers her husband Joey for mouse-removal duty; they will be in the neighbourhood tonight for their daughter's birthday party and will happily stop by.

I decline to accompany them tonight, but promise to go to dinner tomorrow. As we're leaving, I walk across my futon to turn off my reading lamp and spy an envelope leaning against my pillows.

"What," I ask accusingly, "is this?"

She is flustered and babbles a bit:

"I don't know, Joey asked me to drop it off on my way to Andrea's. I was just going to slip it under your door, I didn't know you'd be sitting on your stoop ..."

Scrawled across the front of the envelope:

> Pat
> Writers always can use a little encouragement
> —so here's some for you.
>
> Joey

It's filled with twenties. Nora's watching me, she's feeling glad, feeling bad, worried about my reaction.

I'm too tired to sort out what I feel, but I worry about her worrying, so I smile my gratitude, which is real enough though not unencumbered. The moment passes and we're on our way to Dooney's coffee shop.

-.-.-

I am concerned about the loans and gifts and dinners.

I don't want other people to be negatively affected by me. I don't want people worrying. It threatens me, threatens my autonomy. Because when people care about you they tend to ask questions, make suggestions and perhaps even interfere in your life.

I am aware that under the current Mental Health Act, by the questions psychiatrists pose in order to assess whether the subject is a danger to self or others, I could have been deemed certifiable from time to time. And the cure?

Medical welfare, a drug card, a prescription and perhaps another room in another boarding home, where all my needs would be met.

—.—.—.—

A week has gone by, and my books are still piled in the middle of my floor. I no longer feel entitled to them.

In another week, I won't even be entitled to the floor. Another rent day looms.

—.—.—.—

TORIES TO REPEAL LAW ON ELDERLY, DISABLED

The provincial government will repeal the Advocacy Act by the end of the year but vows to continue protecting the "vulnerable people" for whom the law was designed.

Only four months old, the act created the Advocacy Commission to provide rights advice and assign advocates to represent elderly and disabled people, primarily those in provincial institutions.

But Marilyn Mushinski, minister for citizenship, culture and recreation, said in a news release yesterday that the Advocacy Act "is a costly, complex and overly bureaucratic approach" to meeting the needs of the elderly and disabled.

Former New Democrat MPP David Reville, who heads the Advocacy Commission, said he was "disappointed" by yesterday's announcement.

(Daniel Girard, *Toronto Star*, July 27, 1995)

"Look," David says, pointing to a fellow at the table in front of us who's holding a sheaf of papers he occasionally scribbles something on. "He's working on a manuscript."

I'd confessed, on the way here, that I'd always longed to write in the open air of Dooney's patio, but was prevented by self-consciousness: I'd feel pretentious as hell.

David had suggested, "You could put up a sign, 'It's non-fiction.'"

"How can you tell it's a manuscript?" I ask, squinting at the typed pages with many ink revisions.

"Because it says 'Chapter 2' on top."

I take his word for it.

"So he's well-adjusted. Lord, I hope I don't have to make

that many changes with the new book. I hate rewrites."

Our omelettes, with toast and homefries, and the carton of cigarettes David has brought me on the side, arrive just as we're finishing our café au lait. This is my first real breakfast in some time, and I am determined to enjoy every bite of it.

I haven't seen David since the dinner party Nora gave me as a belated birthday event. He'd seemed unnaturally subdued then.

"It was one of those stay-in-the-house-and-hide days," he confesses. "But it was for you, so I had to go. I wasn't sure how you were going to take it, I was sure you'd hate the idea of it. But you were pretty cool."

"Initially, I was cringing, but I got over it."

I am learning what a tyrant I appear to my friends. Nora was advised by a few of them that I'd get angry if she really did give this party. But I am used, now, to dinner parties at the Slingers', and went unsuspecting to this barbecue, expecting to see the usual array of interesting folks that I'm too nervous to talk to.

"Then Cathy was mad, because I'd gotten you cigarettes, so I worried about that, you know. Were people supposed to be giving you Tupperware? After, Cathy said we should have got you two cartons."

"No argument from me," I grinned at him.

I get down to business, having finished with my plate.

"I want to know how it feels not to have a job, just by itself, without the added burden of poverty or illness. I know it's been hard on you, and I think it's important people understand how corrosive it is, even when you have a financial safety net."

He nods, looking off down the street, marshalling

his thoughts.

I first met him when he was junior alderman for Ward 7, back when I lived in the psychiatric boarding home in Parkdale, on medical welfare, struggling to keep my head above water. He then went on to be MPP for Riverdale, senior adviser to Premier Rae and finally chair of the short-lived Ontario Advocacy Commission, on which I sat. He was kept on in that role up till four months ago, to oversee the dismantling.

"I guess what strikes me most is the reappearance of feelings I thought were far behind me. You know, you're a screw-up, you've always been a screw-up, so where else should you be but here? You swallow a lot of blame. I spend a lot of time wondering where I made my mistakes, should I have done this or that."

He has a striking physical presence, especially now, in his early fifties. He's determined to give me an honest account of his emotions, even as they still have a hold on him.

"There are days when I go for walks around the city, and I look at all the people, all the working people, and I feel horribly envious. I sit on a streetcar and get jealous of the driver. He's got a job. I have to talk to myself: 'You wouldn't be happy doing that.'"

We both light up. I am remembering, about fifteen years ago, David telling me that the best thing about making a salary, when he most appreciated it, was in winter, waiting at a bus stop for a bus that wouldn't come and being able to casually flag down a cab.

I remember too his eyes filling with tears after I'd been working at PARC long enough to get a bank card, when we both withdrew money from the automatic teller.

"Isn't it great?" he'd said, watching me, like a proud father, as I stuffed twenties in my pocket.

"Some days are devastating. Nothing will ever go right again. Nothing I'm trying to do makes sense. And of course all your friends fill you with advice, some of it good, some of which makes you want to scream. It's better lately, but it still depends on the day, how you wake up feeling."

He's trying to make a go of David Reville and Associates, a consultancy office. Touching all the bases, doing the networking, the mailouts, the phone calls.

"The hardest thing is keeping your sense of self, that you still are who you were. I don't fear poverty, that's some years away. I fear loss of self."

We start talking about gradations of poverty—the ease of student poverty, which he, like many, experienced. His father was a judge in a small town, conferring instant status on his family. He didn't do without, until university. Even after he stopped being a student, it was the hippie days, and being poor seemed almost natural.

I nod to that, feeling a rush of nostalgia. "It was in the mental hospital that I found out what it was to live with nothing at all."

And then, in the blink of an eye, a wife and two babies, a succession of low-paying, fast-disappearing jobs, mounting bills, arguments that escalated, a ruthless grinding down of hope, of expectations. Those memories stay with you, haunt you. They define his need for rootedness, for stability, for family.

"Tell me, David, what keeps you going, through the bad days?"

"I believe, I really believe, that if I just keep working, day after day, just keep at it, no matter how futile it can seem, I'll make it through to the other side."

"Isn't that the middle-class promise, the social pact, that's supposed to be dead? Work hard, get ahead?"

"Not for me. Not dead for me. Maybe it's a middle-class thing. I don't know. But it's worked for me before, it's what I know."

I wonder how he's kept the trust, when all around him he can see it's not happening for people, people like him.

But I wonder silently.

I was never imbued with that ethic, never looked for the payoff. Though I understand the meaning of home and marriage and career to him, it is more of an academic than empathetic understanding.

I'd like good work and a fair salary, but hold the trimmings, please.

—.—.—

I couldn't continue accepting handouts, no matter how generously offered. Couldn't also have people worrying. Friends suggested I make a start towards "real" employment, so I took the path of least resistance and made a call to Laurie Hall, the director of A-way Express Couriers.

A-way is a consumer/survivor business: couriers with a history of mental illness on some form of social assistance who ride the public transit system throughout the city delivering envelopes and packages. It doesn't pay much, in terms of cash, but since everyone is on welfare or disability, they're not allowed to earn much. There's more to it than money. Self-esteem, for one; companionship, for another. And soon, I'm told, a softball team.

I did my two days of training, constantly aware of the level of empathy and sensitivity and humour of these members of my community. I confess to dreading the first delivery to one of the more regressive mental health agencies or hospitals, and I determined to adopt a steely glare when necessary. Otherwise, it's been fun, though the pay is less than flipping burgers, and the shifts are under five hours, three days a week.

My optimist says: it's a start.

RESIDENTS AMONG WORLD'S HEALTHIEST

Vancouver—British Columbians are among the healthiest in the world—except for natives, the poor and the less educated.

The overall life expectancy of 79 years is second only to Japan and higher than the Canadian average. However, that figure drops by five years in poor parts of the province and by 12 years for aboriginals.

"We've reached the point where you can think of poverty and low income the way in the past that we've thought of smoking," health officer Dr. John Millar said yesterday after releasing his 1995 report on B.C. health.

"It's [as] causally related to people's poor health as smoking and lung cancer. It's that solid."

Health improves with every step up in income, education and employment, he said....

Lifestyles also affect health but to a lesser degree than socioeconomic factors.

(Globe and Mail, **March 5, 1996)**

—.—.—

The only exercise my canary gets, aside from plummeting to the floor when he tries to fly, is balancing on my shoulder and pecking at my earlobe while I pace. This week the humidity is extreme, and my room is barely tolerable, for him or me, though he gets to stand in his birdbath more frequently than my once-daily immersion in the bathtub. As much as I dread the onslaught of winter, I will be glad to see the end of summer. Not that I saw that much of it, only the downside of soaring temperatures filtered through the small, solitary window screen facing my street.

I close my eyes and catch a memory: July 1st weekend, up at my friend Cynthia Good's cottage. A birthday present from her to me.

At 5:15 a.m., I'm down at the dock, thermos and breakfast at hand, deck chair unfolded, book open, all without waking her up.

I'm feeling very efficient, but also very much like a Chernobyl kid brought out to Canada for a breath of fresh air, conscious of time ticking away, alive in the moment only. Thinking of those left behind.

It's so early the sun and I are eye to eye for a while, and I grin at it across the lake. No power boats, no canoes, just calm water, and a dazzling variety of birds achieving a kind of melodious, rising harmony. I wonder at the first splash or two I hear, but then catch sight of fish, feeding and blowing bubbles and occasionally jumping right out of the water. I might be forgiven for feeling all this is for my benefit, staged exclusively for me.

I pour my coffee, unwrap the various slices of cake Cynthia brought from a family affair, light a cigarette and experience a total, overwhelming sense of well-being.

"Let them eat cake," I whisper, in a peculiar benediction, taking a bite. Today I won't worry about hunger. The dock rocks ever so gently on the water, underlining the peace of the morning. I hear the distant call of a loon. Cynthia has told me they are on the lake though she hasn't seen one yet.

We've been friends since she drove me back from Penguin's sales conference, after I'd addressed their sales reps about *Upstairs in the Crazy House*, in 1991. She is the publisher at Penguin Books Canada. A few months later I persuaded her to join the Gerstein Centre's board of directors.

She is very different from the other important people in my life: totally apolitical, unabashedly religious and an absolute enjoyer of life (when it's going well). She is generous in heart and spirit, cries freely when watching sad movies, loves baseball and (okay, everyone has faults) listens to the New Country

Music. We talk about religion, philosophy, political correctness, what makes for normality, books and life.

The cottage is a relatively new acquisition, but it's a smart one. A few weeks ago she had a small deck added on, where she's set up the barbecue. She promised to make whatever I wanted for supper, and, being a pleb, I asked for hamburgers.

The plopping of another surfacing fish draws me back, and the loon calls again, closer this time, off to my left. The lake bends and disappears from view into the trees leaning out over the water.

Again the call. Like a herald. Indeed, just like a herald, for here he comes, majestically borne forth, slow ripples ahead of him, no effort at all on his part. He has all my attention, and I have to remind myself to breathe. He waits till he's almost in the centre of the lake and calls again.

I want to applaud, but just whisper again: *Very cool, very, very cool.*

It's a day, a morning when God doesn't feel so far off, and I accept the moment like a balm, a touch of peace, a flicker of light, as the first motorboat of the day powers up, and the loon takes flight.

hen I left the psychiatric boarding home and welfare for a job at PARC, I rented the bottom floor of a duplex in Parkdale; it had a real kitchen, a real fridge and stove, two bedrooms, a large bathroom, and a living room. Lots of windows, too. But I couldn't stretch myself so thin, to fill up all the space. I tried to make one room into a study, tried to sit in the kitchen to eat, tried to sleep in the bedroom, but it was too much, too vast. I ended up living, sleeping, eating, writing, reading in the living room, ignoring every other space but the bathroom. I didn't stay there long. I started joking to my friends that I was looking for a detached room, but it wasn't really a joke.

In many ways, this room is ideal for me. But the drawbacks to the place are very real, such as the landlord's tendency to believe no one needs heat during the day in winter. I gave up nagging him and bought a space-heater, but that kept shorting out the fuses, so now I just stay cold.

And the tiny amount of air that comes in through the part of the window that opens is equally frustrating. And the mice, of course.

But it's quiet, and fairly clean, it's a nice neighbourhood, and nobody bugs me. I don't step over huddled bodies when I go out, the way I had to when I lived on Jarvis, or when I lived off Gerrard. I'm not afraid to go out at night. I don't jump at every noise the way I used to.

I accused myself of hiding from reality when I first moved here: everything was so clean in the area, and the conversations I would overhear in coffee shops and restaurants were vacuous at worst, pretentious at best. The life in the neighbourhoods I'd left behind seemed more vital, if more desperate.

Now, though, instead of a hooker who still hasn't lost her baby fat framed in my window, there's a schoolyard with children running and shouting and at least seeming to be happy. I forgave my need to run away from the constant onslaught of the misery around me. I made my peace with the neighbourhood, and my place in it.

The fridge is tricky, not quite cold enough for milk or meat over a twenty-four-hour period. I'm fortunate, too, that I have only mice and not roaches, the most secure tenants in most "affordable" housing.

–.–.–

TAUNTS HURLED AT TSUBOUCHI OVER WELFARE SHOPPING LIST

*MPPs call on minister to live on bland diet
of bologna and beans*

Toronto—Ontario's welfare recipients have been given a shopping list from their Social Services Minister, a guide for spending only $90.21 a month on food, while existing on an unforgivingly bland diet of such things as bologna, canned beans, and pasta without sauce....

Almost no one lives on just the items on the list, which was created by one of Mr. Tsubouchi's staff members for a single person on welfare, who currently receives $195 a month for living expenses other than rent.

The list contains only one head of lettuce a month and one can of orange juice. It has no salad dressing, coffee, tea, condiments, sugar, butter, sweets or junk food, the type of things most people eat.

The City of North York Public Health Department estimated in July that a realistic monthly food bill for a single male 25 to 49 years old would be $156 a month, 73 percent more than Mr. Tsubouchi's shopping basket.

A check by *The Globe and Mail* of the items at a

downtown [store] found it was possible to buy
the minister's grocery basket for $87.81, a
few dollars under budget....

But a more realistic list, including sugar,
margarine, soft drinks, pasta sauce, mayonnaise, ketchup and oil added another $20.40.
Some commonly used items, such as toothpaste, freezer bags, soap, detergent and shampoo, added another $16.93 before tax.

(Martin Mittelstaedt, with a report from
Jane Gadd, *Globe and Mail*, October 21, 1995)

Most single people living at or near the welfare level are
likely to be living in rooming houses or their equivalent. They
might, in a best-case scenario, have a hot plate, although most
places ban them as a fire hazard. They might have shared access
to a kitchen, but they're likely to have whatever they try to
store ripped off by the less frugal.

I am fortunate, in that I have a toaster oven and a bar-sized
fridge, as well as a plug-in kettle/pot that can cook soup.

I kept track of my own diet through the month of June, on
those days when there was food to eat, and it consisted primarily of bagels, pink grapefruit (three for a dollar for a while),
peanut-butter-and-banana sandwiches, tomato sandwiches,
baked potatoes with salsa, nachos with salsa (spicy, it leaves you
feeling fuller), English cucumber, an occasional apple and hot
dogs.

I should be clear that I didn't have all of the above available at the same time. I might be eating plain bagels every day for a week, then three days of pink grapefruit, four days of tomato sandwiches (with mayonnaise but no lettuce or margarine), another week of peanut-butter-and-banana sandwiches, three days of hot dogs and weekends with cucumber in vinegar. Eating would be confined to the morning (otherwise the acidic content of the coffee destroyed my stomach) and as late in the evening as possible.

In between, of course, great amounts of tap water. Three cups of coffee a day, with Coffeemate and Sugar Twin.

I confess, I didn't spend a lot of time worrying about nutrition, just volume enough to quell hunger pangs.

I am more fortunate than most of the chronically poor, in that I have more contact with the other classes. It would be rare indeed for a single mother on social assistance in Regent Park to get an invitation to dinner parties or literary events or summer cottages. Rarer still to get periodic offers of cash or groceries delivered to her door. The poor are usually as confined by their poverty as if they lived in a maximum-security prison. There is not much exposure to other ways of life, unless their neighbourhood starts to undergo gentrification. And since all the rents go up once that happens, they have to then move on to somewhere not so attractive to the "yuppie" element. There is no relief, no temporary respite, such as I have enjoyed from time to time.

It's been seven months since I signed on to do this book. A small advance helped me to pay back loans and ensure a few more months of housing. It didn't do much to mitigate poverty. I make jokes about how different poverty feels when you can claim to be a starving artist.

For instance, last year, around Christmas. It's a holiday I've come to hate, for what it does to those who have to endure it, have to hear what a joyful time it is while they huddle in misery. As a volunteer and as a worker, I've helped to dish out Christmas dinners, helped to try to alleviate a time that seems only to emphasize abandonment and poverty. It's a time I prefer to spend alone, even under the best economic conditions, and to resolutely ignore. And yet:

On December 22, I was picked up and driven to a party where I ate lasagna and baked beef salami.

On December 23, friends took me to a movie and a Chinese buffet.

On December 24, I ate a gift of shortbread cookies which left me with, on the 25th, a can of whole potatoes that I strained and sprinkled with spice from my previous life and warmed in my toaster oven.

WELFARE DIET "DEPRESSED" TESTERS, LEFT SOME OF THEM LACKING ENERGY

The feeling was unanimous among participants.

Trying to live within Social Services Minister David Tsubouchi's new welfare requirements— even if it was just for a week—was not easy.

And sometimes it was downright horrible....

"I don't want to have a tax cut if it means people on welfare are going to have their income cut further," [Dr. Debbie] Honickman said.

[Nurse Kimberly] Enright said the experience left her feeling "closed in," giving her insight into a "very boring and demeaning" way to live. East York Mayor Prue said it was "a gut-wrenching experience" that left him not only physically hungry but lethargic and even a little aggressive....

[*Globe and Mail* business writer David] Olive said that while he had always preached fiscal restraint in his columns, the awareness of how difficult it was to look for work on an empty stomach hit home for him.

(Phinjo Gombu, *Toronto Star*, November 11, 1995)

Allow me to chronicle some of my own findings after a year of poverty diets.

Chronic fatigue is a definite, without the possible disability benefit of the critical add-on: "syndrome."

Generalized feelings of anxiety.

Lowered immunity to coughs, colds and whatever else is going around. Constant headaches. Difficulty concentrating. Difficulty sleeping. An annoying tendency to linger over television cooking shows. Limp hair. Sallow complexion. Slight tremor in the hands.

Acute sensitivity to cold. Lowered frustration tolerance.

I coped, in my way. I was lucky enough to have a whole bottle of suntan lotion left over from the summer, so that, during the warm months, I could cover my paleness with a healthy-looking tan.

And, since everybody seems to want to lose weight, for a while I could be tanned and lean without worrying anybody. My problem was with my jeans. Much earlier, I felt I had matured enough to reach an accommodation with my weight, so I had settled for a few pairs of Levi's in size 34, and a couple of pairs in an optimistic size 33. I couldn't wear any of these now without alarming people. I had to search my belongings to come up with a single pair of 32s, which were also now hanging off me, in spite of frequent soaking in hot water to try and shrink them.

I hate the thought of public neediness, which these jeans seemed to shout—a worse giveaway than a growling stomach, which I also constantly fall prey to.

I still believe I can handle almost everything, as long as it is known to me alone. I don't want to be a public concern.

Headaches are another difficult side effect of hunger. Aspirin gets to be a luxury that has to be lived without, but I fear headaches, which can easily become migraines. I try to cope the best I can with hot and cold cloths, but there are times those solutions fail, and those are very bad times.

For someone as prone to depression as I am, very bad times are bad indeed.

I couldn't see any light at the end of the tunnel, couldn't see any way that I would make it out of the situation I found myself in.

I felt I was there as long as I could endure it. And when it's forever, unlike the good folks who tried it for a week, you can't look forward to its ending. There is only getting through today and tomorrow and the next day, all the days carbon copies of each other.

Except for my geriatric canary, I live alone. I cannot imagine what it's like to be hungry and worn out physically and emotionally, and still have to deal with children and their needs. And also the guilt that comes from not being able, often, to supply even the basics. There are days when my nerves are so frayed, just from the supreme effort of keeping myself together, from lack of sleep, from a kind of cabin fever, that I thank God I have no one dependent on me.

Poverty, for many, is a life sentence, with no hope of parole.

And, as Mr. Harris has shown, things can always get worse.

e's willing to give credit where credit's due. Harris motivated him. Before that, he'd been, if not content, at least accepting of his $800(ish)-a-month lifestyle, the sum paid by the province to those considered permanently disabled.

"But you listen to the guy, how he talks, you watch what he's doing to people, and you wonder, who's next, you know?"

He's had his hair professionally styled, and it looks good. He's a strange mix of urchin and angel. He flourished a huge bouquet at my door, begging forgiveness for being late. I remind him that he's doing me the favour, submitting to this interview. We'd spent some time previously, analyzing the risk he would be taking, and I found that I was more worried than him. We'll call him Richard.

He borrows my phone to call his backed-up clients, warning each that he's running about an hour and a half behind. No one hassles him. He gets the phone numbers he needs from his pager and the names from his computer notebook. He ought to be Entrepreneur of the Year.

Richard was born in Toronto's west end, raised by his mother after the death of a father he doesn't really remember. He sloughs off any notion of hardship in his childhood, or poverty memories.

"We made out okay, my mother did the best she could. Wasn't easy." An understatement: widowed, in her twenties, with a handful of kids.

He rolls a large joint, confiscating my (Hilroy) notebook for a flat surface. I don't have what I think of as real furniture in my room. I have a large futon, which doubles, triples really, as a table, a couch and a bed. There is one chair, an uncomfortable office-type chair I use when I'm at my computer.

I sit at one end of the bed, he at the other, and I wait patiently, and with some anticipation, for him to light the joint and give me back my book. There is no set form to plow through, no pre-established list of questions. I like to go wherever his first few answers take me, and I sidetrack myself a bit with listening to stories of his early sexual experiences.

He doesn't really remember not knowing he was gay. When he tells me his first experience was with an older man, a neighbour he calls his "mentor," I say it sounds more like pedophilia to me. He laughs, and says he was "already dicking around" with members of his gang, kids he hung around with, all firmly hetero now.

He was officially diagnosed HIV-positive in May 1986.

(My ageing canary, having clearly inhaled, rips out an impressive series of warbles and hops a little closer.)

"It wasn't a big surprise, I kind of suspected."

I ask him when he'd first heard of AIDS; he thinks back, maybe 1985. He remembers a friend telling him there was this bad disease, that at least fourteen people in Canada already had it.

"But it seemed really far way, you know? Bad shit, but happening somewhere else."

Until the dying started, all around him. A lover, friends.

Not easy, being working class, being gay. Really not easy, in the same setting, being HIV-positive. He wanted to go home for a while; he had no idea how fast he would be affected, how fast AIDS would get him. It took him a long time, getting up the courage to tell his mother.

"She knew before I did. We never talked about it, but she worried."

His siblings were harder, especially one sister who demanded he stay away from her children. That's hard to forget.

He didn't have many options open to him. He'd never been interested in school, or school in him, for that matter. The jobs he'd been able to get were mostly unskilled, low-paying, physically demanding and didn't come with the benefits he'd need to cover his medication costs. He believed that kind of work would kill him faster. He considered it better, wiser, to go on the provincial disability pension. He didn't want to die.

Except for that time in 1989, when he "crawled into a plastic bag, lay there on the floor," having no heart for the protracted battle he saw before him. Friends broke in, took him to hospital. He tried overdosing the next night, which bought him a week on a psychiatric ward. He's not a kid to be kept down. Essentially optimistic, a lover of life, I can't find any trace of anger or bitterness in him.

He's not political at all. He's taking time out from his business to go to the AIDS conference in Vancouver—not to attend, but because of all the beautiful men who'll be gathered there. (Yes, Virginia, there is still safe, informed sex after HIV.)

He has all the hi-tech doodads available to his profession. An electronic scale, his computer notebook, his pager. He buys the small plastic bags wholesale, after calculating the savings he'll earn. As for starting the business, it was like buying a franchise, he tells me. He only had to pay for the name of the supplier. Proudly, he tells me he didn't have to purchase a client list, having effectively established a growing word-of-mouth customer base.

His pager goes off periodically during the interview, and he makes the necessary calls, giving estimates of how long he'll be. My usually stand-offish canary seems to want to snuggle up to him, seems to be wagging his tail, as he rolls yet another, as I struggle to keep on track.

"I get these guys who tell me, 'Richard, I deserve a discount, look how many people I've referred to you.'" He presses a few buttons. "So I go into this file, and I can see exactly how many he's sent, whether he's trying to scam me or not."

He's proud of the computer he's been able to buy, and he goes into enormous, technical detail about it. I'm impressed. But then again, if he hadn't figured out how to fix my computer when it refused to do anything but beep alarmingly at me, I never would have finished the "Dear Mr. Harris" piece. He's proud of that, too. As proud as I am grateful.

These are the things that keep him going. The friends he can help, the travelling he can do, the smoke that calms him. The food he can buy, the kind of food you don't get on a disability diet but that's so essential to fending off full-blown AIDS.

And all the people he meets, day to day, on his appointed rounds. He's very much a people person.

His customer base is mostly middle-class men and women, between thirty and fifty years old, gainfully employed, educated, articulate. Though it's not exactly thirty minutes or free, it's close enough, and it beats hell out of approaching street dealers, or sitting around a strange house, waiting nervously for a quarter ounce to be measured out, starting at every noise in the hall. A discreet, personable fellow who delivers. Yuppie heaven.

He tells me he knows he should get off disability, but it would feel like tearing up an insurance policy. He can't save money, they check bank accounts, so he spends what he earns and celebrates the day.

I believe I have learned about class distinctions, seen the lines even as I crossed them. People are essentially people—what matters most is what they're like inside. I've met dreadful men and women on either side of the spectrum, as well as shiningly decent people, the courageous, the gracious, the infinitely patient....

Though I know it's unlikely they'll connect in Vancouver— there will be too many "beautiful people"—I show Richard a picture of a friend of mine, an AIDS activist who's worked on the planning committee for the conference.

Tony told me that he used to be a fairly disgusting suburban yuppie, not involved in the gay community, living the good life with his lover, making big bucks as a developer. Till his lover was diagnosed with AIDS, and he came up against a system that blew his mind. He has spent the last ten years fighting to make a difference; he's on more committees and boards than he has names in his little black book.

He's watched as Harris dismantles most of the gains his community has made, including issuing threats to a hospital in the gay community that's made an extraordinary difference in the lives of those suffering from AIDS. He shares with me a fierce independence that's now threatened. He too is HIV-positive, and he used to point out to me the future site of the housing that promised him death with dignity and intact autonomy, a subsidized two-bedroom for himself and a live-in caregiver so he could avoid institutionalization, which has, after two years of planning and proposals and a final go-ahead, fallen prey to the Harris cuts.

I wonder how he sees his tomorrows now; I wonder if he sleeps at night. I wonder what his T-cell count is.

can't afford to buy newspapers every day, not even the weekend *Globe and Mail* any more. So I might not have seen the article or, even if I had, it might not have bothered me as much if I hadn't heard Ms. Wong interviewed several times, on radio and television, around the anniversary of the massacre at Tiananmen Square, because she'd been there, because she had a book out. I liked the things she said, the perspective she brought.

A number of people drew my attention to the piece; it was hard to miss, being on the front page.

Some excerpts:

In a month, she may collect anywhere from $500 to $900 tax-free, in addition to the

$900 cheque the government sends her and her husband....

[She] and her husband live in a one-bedroom apartment that costs them a government-subsidized $225 a month. "With a balcony," she said emphatically....

Although she has only three teeth left, "I can still eat steak, corn-on-the-cob," she said. Her only extravagances are an occasional mickey of rum, a pack-a-day cigarette habit and cable television. She buys the deluxe package—Bravo, Disney, TSN, which costs about $60 a month.

[She] begs from her $4,000 Ultramatic wheel-chair-scooter, which the government gave her in 1992 after she injured her back in a fall....

Asked whether she is actually disabled, she hesitated.

"Yes and no," she said. She acknowledged that she can walk, and say, carry groceries. At first glance she seems disabled, perhaps because she rarely moves and because she carries 274 pounds on her four-foot-eleven frame....

She has never worked a day in her life....

Unlike her counterparts in the United States, she would never dream of being pushy. She was horrified to hear about a San Francisco beggar who, when turned down by a patron at a sidewalk café, retaliated by grabbing the person's sandwich.

"That's rude," [she] said. Why, she herself has been in a restaurant, having a coffee and a doughnut, counting up the loose change she has collected. "You're trying to relax, and someone hits up on me for a smoke or some money."

And does she ever give?

"Never. I say, I'm trying to make money for myself. I say, I got two babies at home. That's how I think of my two dogs."

(Jan Wong, "Charity pays off on Canada's kind streets," *Globe and Mail*, May 27, 1996)

I don't question the accuracy of Wong's piece, rather its selectivity, the lack of any real effort at balance and its prominence in Canada's national newspaper. Her moral outrage is barely contained by the paragraphs she writes. And clearly, at least 52 percent of this province's voters agree with her tone, and agree with the "hang 'em high" solution offered up by Premier Harris. It's reflected in his consistently high approval rating.

It's not that I don't understand the impulse to blame, to stereotype, to divide people into the worthy and the unworthy poor. It salves and irritates at the same time, this burning sense of the taxpayer as the true victim.

My brother Michael caused me to react in such a way to his plight.

We both started from the same lousy place, we both made choices all down the line. I was responsible for mine—wasn't he for his?

I had so much, or, more to the point, so little left to give the population I had chosen to speak with and for—I was entitled to preserve it, wasn't I? For the "true victims"?

We can understand, most of us, how it is that many sons of powerful fathers spend their lives in shadow, never quite feeling as though they've measured up. In an upside-down, inside-out way, my brother suffered from this syndrome. While he and my sisters and I huddled round the bedroom door listening to screams and the sounds of fists battering flesh and bone, while we sisters were identifying with the victim, he was feeling the power of his role model.

Even when it was his turn to be battered and kicked and humiliated, something in him admired the strength and rage that victimized him. He made no conscious connection years later to his own beating of his girlfriends, to his obsession with weight-lifting, to the same empty racist and homophobic remarks he'd breathed in like oxygen all through his childhood.

If asked, he'd deny any abuse as such.

"Children need discipline."

I remember when he was just entering his teenage years, our father learned, on one of his furious inspections of our rooms, that his son was still wetting his bed, or, more to the point, still ruining his mattress. He needed to be shamed out of his laziness, so his sisters were lined up at the bottom of the stairs to witness the humiliation. He was forced to take off his clothes and carry his stained mattress from his room, past his family, outside to the back yard. While his father screamed abuse at him, and fists fell on his head and shoulders. *Children need discipline.*

He grew up a frightening young man. Hypersensitive to criticism, real or implied. He never had many friends.

It would be reasonable to expect that he might emulate his father, and he did try, but he'd never learned the first rule: keep violence in the home.

He found a job he could thrive at, and if circumstances had been different, he might still be working there, have married and had children of his own.

His job involved finding other people's mistakes, in packaging quality control: he could tell other people, in various ways, that they were stupid. His live-in girlfriend had a job at the same pharmaceutical firm. He hit her one time too many at work, and he was fired. He called my mother and screamed at her: "Call her, explain to her! Make her drop her complaint!" (*"You know the rules of the game, make her follow them!"*) His angry response to his mother's failure to intervene was to disappear for years.

He never really worked again. He tried, but the jobs he got were manual labour, and someone was always "out to get him." He went on welfare, smoked a lot of dope and lifted weights.

He looked for opportunities to use his fists, or other weapons he carried from time to time. He'd leave his bike leaning, unlocked, against a wall, while he stood in the shadows and waited for someone to try and steal it. He only ever talked about one thing: his job, successes he'd had, making the firm recall defective pill containers, representing his peers at the union level.

On occasion, a battered woman would show up at one or another of my sisters' homes, saying, "Look what your brother did."

He cut off everyone who'd try to talk to him about his behaviour.

Then, after years of silence, he called from his hospital bed.

My sisters and I were in the room with him when the doctor confirmed his fears that he had full-blown AIDS. It was a Roy Cohn moment: leprosy would have been easier for him to accept. It didn't matter what we said—he felt profound shame. He blamed one of the girls we'd met—a coke-addled model he'd gone with for years, beaten up for years—but we shrugged and said that wasn't the point. The point was he was very sick, not how he got sick.

He survived the first bout with pneumonia, applied for disability and moved into a room. It was harder to see him there than in the hospital. It was hard to know I did not love him, did not like him. It was incredibly difficult to try and have a conversation with him. He was so empty. My sisters took over when I fell back, cooking for him, ensuring his rent was paid, while I tried to justify not seeing him. I'd send him things, and money, but I could not bring myself to see him face to face.

The frustration, the guilt, the great, aching, useless pity that overwhelmed me when I was still visiting him, for all he could have been and all he was, were enormously destructive. I couldn't sleep. I felt as though I'd entered a Stephen King universe where the sins of the father continued to claim their victims. All his sisters understood the cost of standing by this young man. Dianne, the closest to him in age, fought the hardest for him, throwing off her own fears, memories of him lunging at her in a rage, knife in hand. He was admitted to psychiatric wards, partly from the consequences of using inhalants to escape his nightmares, partly from a mass forming in his brain. I went back to him, and stayed, like the rest of us, till the end.

Dianne got him into Casey House, and we made pilgrimages to his room, massaging his legs and feet, feeding him, taking him for walks. He refused to break his isolation by sitting "with those people" in the common room. No one visited him except his family, and dear June Callwood, who stopped by his room whenever she was at the hospice. A gift to him and to us. For someone who had never really lived, certainly never loved, he was petrified of dying. It was a blessing for him, and for us, when, after a series of small strokes, he died in his sleep, leaving an emaciated, ruined shell of a body behind.

And we learned, after, that he'd spent the last year of his life with a very sweet man, well known in the gay community, who hadn't dared talk to us while Michael was still alive, for fear of his violent reaction. That was a bitter-sweet revelation: that he might have been able to give and receive love, and that shame prevented him from sharing that reality.

Aside from shame, the biggest fear he'd had of AIDS was his

vulnerability: he had nightmares of being chased by crowds of men, kicked and beaten, and worst of all, not having the strength to fight back.

I learned that suffering is suffering, need is need, and the cost of turning righteously away from the sufferer is a worse loss of self than the consequences of trying to alleviate that suffering.

Nothing he did in his life, nothing he'd allowed himself to become, justified turning away. So while I understand very well the impulse to say, *he is undeserving*, when we start saying that, when we start making those choices, there is no stopping. Until the streets are filled with everyone we've so categorized. Until the day we find ourselves numbered among them.

This is what the poor, the disabled and the elderly are learning from one another: better to teach than to hate; better to talk than turn away; better to see another human being in trouble than to deny your humanity; better to remember I may be just a handicap away from being you.

Even in extremes, I'm trying to reach you.

Ms. Wong's article got a new lease on life when CTV's Mike Duffy later used it as proof that the liberal, hand-wringing media have no idea, in their ivory-tower journalism, what's really going on on the streets. He pointed to the polls, the support for Harris, as clear evidence that the people aren't fooled. The people know the sky's not falling.

I guess he meant the people that count.

I've been riding the subway more lately, out of necessity, and there are posters up everywhere that begin "FARE CHEATS" and go on to suggest that a person riding for free is cheating everybody who pays their fare. I get a powerful urge, remembering last summer's fatal subway crash in Toronto, to make my own poster, or buy a can of spray paint, and print in big letters "SAFETY CHEATS," over a picture of crushed subway cars.

A $2.00 fare.

Human lives.

Of course, there are also the occasional, and well-timed, roundups of welfare cheats that make big headlines. And yet, when savings and loans institutions in the United States were systematically looted by executive directors and board members for awesome amounts of money, how many people do you remember being rounded up, shamed, ordered to make full restitution? Given serious prison sentences?

People on welfare can't afford the same high-priced law firms who helped keep senior federal and provincial bureaucrats from being named and shamed and blamed for all those who contracted the AIDS virus from a "safe" blood supply.

People on welfare can't afford the public relations advisers or spin doctors employed by politicians to put the best face on things; when you're poor, a lie is always a lie. A crime, however petty, however desperate, is always a crime.

The nineties is the decade of the redefinition of the victim. The term has been torn away from those to whom it was first applied and flown as a battle pennant by the tax-paying middle class.

The decade when a courageous bank president can hold his

head almost as high as his profits, and not allow himself to be shamed and victimized any more by bank-bashers.

The decade when Kathy Lee Gifford is the true victim (at least before politically correct public relations advice), not those workers in sweatshops creating her clothing line.

When General Boyle surely feels himself more persecuted than the young Somali boy tortured and beaten to death under his watch.

When former Nova Scotia Premier Cameron becomes comfortably indignant during the Westray Inquiry, and suggests a portion of the blame lies with the dead miners.

Of course there are people who cheat the system. Some much more effectively than others. Some from the underclass, some from the middle class and some from the power elite. There are many more that the system itself has cheated, and continues to cheat.

We live in a time when manipulation of public opinion has been elevated to a science, when stereotypes are accepted as true representatives of their segment of the population. And, as always, stereotypes cause a great deal of pain to those tarred with the same brush. When I read Ms. Wong's article, I knew the pain it would inflict on those already suffering from fear and shame and the increasing stigma of need.

–·–·–

I am not innocent as far as taking refuge in stereotypes goes. As much as I try to catch myself at it, on occasion I'm forced to admit to myself, and sometimes to others, that I've fallen prey to its comforting lure.

I've served on many committees, task forces, working groups and boards in my seventeen years of mental health advocacy. Before consumer involvement became more widely accepted, I was often the only ex-patient at the table, trying to deal with hospital administrators, bureaucrats, psychiatrists, nurses and family groups. I didn't think any board could scare me again, or silence me through intimidation.

I was, however, being forced to admit that one hospital board in particular was giving me a great deal of angst. It left me feeling as though I'd been flung back through time, as though I'd just found the front door to my psychiatric boarding home, and that door was starting to open on a forbidding world.

I used to tell audiences of consumers and mental health staff that one of our biggest problems was that there was no consensus in the system concerning the value of involving clients in the management and delivery of services. One day I'd be working with an agency that possessed the equivalent of New York sophistication around the issues, and the next I'd feel as though I were in Alabama before the civil rights movement got under way.

It wasn't unusual for these opposites to be within a few city blocks of each other.

That was part of my problem with this board, that it was Alabama-like while believing itself to be cutting edge. But there was more. There were deep and obvious class distinctions, and even though I was, at the time, gainfully employed, a published author, someone who possessed the respect of my community, I felt intimidated, looked down on, stereotyped and all the rest. It got so that I had to force myself to attend.

The board was a status board, composed of high-powered bankers, lawyers, publishers and consultants, as well as hospital executives. I was the only one in jeans, in a hat. I was the only one from my particular class and background. I was the only voice expressing criticism of the liberal establishment we were running.

It was dreadful. Meetings were corporate; when I would leave for a cigarette I felt I should be bowing and backing up to the door. Nobody laughed, it seemed, ever. Nobody talked out of turn.

Then, one afternoon when I had screwed up my courage to attend, I bumped into the "fat cat" lawyer in the hallway. He made a joke, and I made one back before I had time to think about it. We both laughed, and I thought we both stared at each other, surprised at the unlikely evidence of a sense of humour beneath the stereotype. Ice got broken. Then the banker who had offered me lifts home before, which I'd declined—what would I have to talk to him about in the car?—offered again, and I accepted. I even teased him about his brand new BMW and the pervasive smell of leather from the seats. He demonstrated how his car phone responded to voice orders to dial numbers, and I confess I got a kick out of the gimmickry. Later, he brought me a novel his wife had enjoyed reading.

I remember another kind of breakthrough event at that board. I was trying once again to explain why I needed more people like me (from my class and experience) around the table. How easy it was to get intimidated in the setting we were in, if you didn't find the corporate air invigorating. How easy it was to dismiss the views I was putting forward because it was only me they were hearing them from. How our class differences, our life experiences, created gulfs between us.

My banker friend took umbrage. He was sure, he said, that he was quite capable of relating to me as a person, as another human being. He felt we were operating on a level playing field, and that I wasn't giving them enough credit.

My lawyer friend then made a remarkable statement.

"That's not true," he said. "Pat didn't start out on a level playing field with me. I took one look at her and summed her up. It wasn't until later that I started to see her differently."

"And I," I said, "did the same thing, summed up you guys at a glance, and what I felt was your attitude towards me. It got easier to walk around with a chip on my shoulder than to try and relate to you."

Even the publisher chimed in:

"I understand what you mean about intimidation. I never saw myself as intimidating, I like to think I'm an easygoing, friendly guy. But some of my staff have been pointing out to me that people who work for me don't have that same picture, because I have power over them. It's not easy or comfortable to realize that you may scare people, but a lot of times it's true."

Only the banker held out for the level playing field precept, but of course the conversation was ruled out of order and we were on to the next item on the agenda.

A month or two later, I decided to transfer my bank account to a branch nearer my residence. To get an account in the first place had been a challenge. I don't have credit cards, or a driver's licence: therefore, I don't have a system-recognized identity.

This is a very common dilemma for those who make up the underclass, and it accounts for the prevalence and huge success of Money Mart cheque-cashing services in poor areas. As long as I've been an advocate, various groups of workers have tried to break through the banking system, to work out generally acceptable ways of identifying clients to tellers through letters of introduction, or special cards, with no real success.

I remember one remarkably honest but still disturbing branch manager who explained his problem to the director of an agency working with chronic psychiatric patients: "I want you to know I'm a Christian man, but I just don't want these people in my bank."

In order for me to get an account in the first place, my publisher, Cynthia Good, had to take me into her branch, where we met with her "personal banking representative," and on the basis of Cynthia's knowledge of me, I got an account in time to deposit the cheque I'd received for the movie rights to my book.

I confess I felt quite mainstream for a while, with my PIN number and cheques and account book, as though I'd arrived. It was enough to make me overconfident. I decided it was silly to travel forty minutes to that branch when there was one a few blocks from me. I still had a balance of a little over $5,000, so I didn't anticipate any problems. I walked into my local branch and was soon seated across from yet another "personal banking representative."

"What can I do for you today?" she asked, pleasantly.

"I'd like to transfer my account to here, please," I responded, handing over my account book and bank card.

"I see, um, would you have some identification?"

I was puzzled.

"Nothing you guys seem to accept. But I only want to transfer, not open, an account."

She persists:

"A major credit card? A driver's licence?"

I have a birth certificate. I remember trying to rent a video using it, and the owner of the store turning the card over and saying, "Your signature's not on it."

I shake my head. I give her the card of the other personal banking representative, the one in whose presence I had been validated.

She phones. She shakes her head. That person is on vacation. She purses her lips, not liking to create difficulties for me, but there are rules.

"I'm sorry, we really do need identification."

I'm getting angry, and I suspect she feels it, which accounts for her visible nervousness. It won't help to get snippy with her. I could just pack it in and leave—it wouldn't be the end of the world, after all. But the battle for reason is under way. It would feel too much like defeat to withdraw now.

I try for a reasoned, measured tone.

"I don't want to withdraw anything. I have $5,000 in my account. You have my card, my cheques, my account book."

I hear steps behind me, I'm sure the security guard is getting ready to pounce.

"It's a different branch of the same bank. C'mon, be reasonable."

"Don't you even have your Indian Status Card?"

"I'm not Indian!"

Ordinarily, I would take it as a compliment, being mistaken

for one of the First People, but in this context, I know there's some heavy stereotyping, and quite possibly some heavy attitude, going on.

I get a flash. I'm terrible about names, remembering names. I can recall the most minute details of conversations, mannerisms, backgrounds and clothing but not names. But I do remember the division my BMW banker is president of. And I do remember it's this same corporation.

I ask her to look up the name of the guy in charge of ———.

"Why?" she asks, immediately suspicious.

"I know him, he can tell you I exist."

Perhaps to humour me, she flips open a book and recites some names.

"That's him," I cry, vindicated. "Give him a call, will you?"

I suppose it's like telling a private to ring up a general at the request of a possible lunatic, an aboriginal impersonator: it's not done.

She excuses herself to consult with a superior. Long minutes pass. I feel myself being examined from the glassed-in cubicles where the decision-makers sit. I feel the breath of the security officer. I feel renewed determination.

She's back.

"I'm sorry about the delay. His secretary had some difficulty reaching him, he's in a meeting. But he is available now."

My understanding smile is as false and strained as her apology.

She picks up the phone and annoyingly turns her chair away from me while she speaks in low tones into the receiver. A few heartbeats, then she passes the phone to me.

Not waiting for his voice, I say:

"I told you there's no level playing field."

He laughs, loudly and honestly.

In under ten minutes, I have my new account, my new card, cheques and a small degree of satisfaction.

Chalk up one for the good guys.

-.-.-

I take refuge in a nearby park, liking and needing the sun and a place to enjoy it. I've checked out the four or five in my neighbourhood, and on days when I need to walk, I go up to the one opposite the Dufferin Mall. I love the solitude, the birds, the green—a perfect setting for reading and tanning.

Picking an empty bench, away from small clumps of people dotting the large park, I open my paperback and disappear into it.

It doesn't seem very long (my watch died a few months ago) before an old fellow, tottering on his cane, shuffles towards me. I look up at his approach, smile briefly and dive back into P. D. James. I am dismayed when he chooses to perch on the other end of my bench, and I try to ignore his presence while my conscience starts bothering me. Now, I only smiled at him because I am aware that some folks think I look a bit tough, and I didn't want him worrying, but he might have mistaken the gesture for a come-chat-with-me invitation. He's probably lonely, isolated, this is probably his big daily outing. Would it kill me to spend a couple of minutes talking to him? Damn.

I close my book, look over at him looking over at me expectantly.

"Beautiful day, isn't it?"

I can barely make out his reply, cloaked in a thick accent, but his head bobbing up and down is pretty clear. I'm stuck for the next sentence, but he keeps going enthusiastically. I make out his name, repeating it triumphantly: "Victor! Hi, I'm Pat."

One arthritic hand grasps mine briefly, then goes back to rest on his cane with the other one.

"I'm retired." He's getting better at speaking clearly, maybe it was just a lack of opportunity that made him rusty. "I was an engineer."

"You live around here?"

He turns painfully, pointing vaguely over his shoulder.

"Right over there, a beautiful place. Very beautiful place."

"Good for you."

I offer him a cigarette, which he accepts, and we sit in companionable silence in the sun. I'm thinking after the smoke I will move on, find another park, maybe nearer my home.

He's talking again, and when I realize what he's saying my jaw drops open.

"If you come see my place, I will give you twenty dollars."

"Jesus Christ! Are you crazy?" I'm so annoyed, and shocked, and thrown off balance by his offer, that I'm blustering. I want to whack him, except he'd probably fall over, like the dirty-old-man character on "Laugh-In."

"Listen to me," I lecture, as I shake a finger in his face. "First off, you're committing a crime. Secondly, it's stupid and dangerous for you. You can't go around offering money to people you don't know for things I don't want to think about. You've insulted me. I could have you arrested! Do you understand?"

Now I'm pretty sure what his daily tour of the park is

about, and I worry about the school-age girls that hang out at lunch time.

"If I see you doing this to anyone else, I will report you, do you get that? I'll be watching you!"

He's stuttering out an apology, which I don't believe, and I refrain from kicking his cane, though I really want to.

On my way home, in between feeling outraged and feeling dirtied, I start to laugh at my own stereotyping of a lonely old man in need of conversation in juxtaposition with his own stereotyping of me.

People ought to wear summing-up signs sometimes, just so you'd know what to expect.

t first glance, Toni can look pretty intimidating, if not off-putting. She wears severe black-framed glasses, hard, nasty-looking shoes and, just lately, a buzz-cut. She explains the cut was a compromise, done on a day when she was struggling against the irresistible urge to do harm to herself, wondering how she could hide yet another cut to her arm. Cutting her hair seemed a reasonable alternative. It used to be shoulder length.

Perhaps, if she could have reached her doctor or her therapist that day, she might not have felt so compelled to do something self-destructive, but life without a phone means sinking or swimming alone through the bad moments.

Self-abuse used to be one of mental health's great mysteries, to psychiatrist and patient alike. It was something I used to engage in, something that got you through those devastating suicidal moments, and it was years before I realized that I wasn't the only one doing this kind of thing. Stopping is almost as hard as giving up smoking, in that there never seems to be an adequate replacement.

Amazingly, she still has a sense of humour about it, and about her life in general.

She's spent two years on medical welfare. Before the latest cuts, she received $649 a month. Now she gets $520.

Her rent: $425.

Hydro: $18.

These are the expenses she feels she can tackle.

I ask her how many days of the month she goes hungry. She laughs. "Every day." She can only afford to eat once a day, so hunger is a constant.

Of course, there are good days—when her parents are in town and take her out to dinner, or when she's asked over to a friend's house, or takes part in a communal church meal. That causes my eyebrows to rise—she doesn't seem like a "churchlady." (I can stereotype with the best of them.)

She grew up in small-town Ontario, and her parents, as far back as she can remember, were always heavily involved in the church, on committees and boards and fund-raisers. She remembers feeling faint discontent, listening to the ministers on Sundays, wanting to become one herself, fairly certain she could do a better job.

She describes herself also as "third-generation Hydro"; her grandfather, father, an uncle and herself all worked for the public utility at one time or another. Her mother concentrated on raising her four children as best she could, and certainly they never felt deprived, though they knew some had it better.

School didn't come easy, however; written work and exams continued to defeat her, though she was never sure why. Her comprehension seemed fine, she was reading above her grade level, but it didn't seem as though university would be in the cards for her. At the time, her sisters and brother seemed happier, better adjusted than she was. She remembers herself as a bit of a schoolyard bully, unhappy, unable to make friends easily. She did get to college, getting herself the necessary papers to get hired on at Hydro, doing work traditionally done by men. She was a workaholic—she had nothing else going on in her life, so work became her sole focus. She loved it.

Eventually, there was an affair with a guy, an unexpected pregnancy, an awareness that this was not a relationship to build on. Her parents offered to help raise the child if she moved back home, but she knew that would be retreating too far. She went through the painful process of giving the child up for adoption.

"For a long time after that, I went around looking for a pre-fab family, you know, a guy with kids I could help raise, and sure enough, along comes this fellow with two kids and a job, who says he loves me, and I thought I loved him. I knew I loved the kids. We got married, and poof, there I was, a legiti-mate mom."

The marriage soon soured, however, as her husband began to reveal an abusive nature.

"He would constantly put me down. He'd force me to do things I didn't want to do, sexually. It didn't matter what I wanted, or what I felt like, you know? Anyway, that's what triggered things for me: how I'd feel after being forced. And I started weirding out. I wasn't sure what was happening."

In an effort to escape the weirdness going on inside her head, she accepted work transfers to North Bay, Oakville and finally Toronto, desperate to get clear, to have a new beginning. She was worried about the possibility of a brain tumor, or a strange form of epilepsy.

She'd space out at work—work that involved high-voltage connections. When she'd come back to herself, she'd find she'd continued to work although with no awareness, and she'd have to recheck everything. She scared herself so badly, she knew she had to quit.

Now she was alone, unemployed and scared in the big city. For someone who had used work to fill and form her life, who was used to feeling competent and independent at least in that aspect of her days, long idleness and stillness meant more time for her past to catch up and overwhelm her.

There are words that summon up comfortable, soft, pleasant images: puppy, kitten, mom, grandfather. "Walton" kinds of words. Toni's grandfather was an important figure in her life. He loomed large as someone who was always there for her, someone who cared for her as she cared for him. He even paid for her college tuition. She looks sick remembering this.

And now this discordant echo, this distortion, amplified and destructive and upside down. A memory abruptly surfaced one day—a memory of her grandfather sexually abusing her—and she was devastated.

She did have some luck during this time in Toronto. An extraordinary doctor—sensitive, empathetic and interested—encouraged Toni to talk to at least one of her sisters, and when she did, she was relieved and horrified to learn she wasn't crazy, wasn't delusional. He'd abused others. And she herself was not the cause, even if, in a secret part of her, it would always feel that way.

But there was even more to uncover. Not quickly, not all at once. She and her sister wanted to blow the whistle: they told their parents; their mother begged them not to. She herself was assaulted with her own long-buried memories, of her father's sins, her father's hands.

He was a predator, thriving in the silence he demanded of his victims. His own child, his child's children. And Toni wonders, who else, in this community, who else?

They went for family counselling. "We got closer. We worked through a lot." But still, the questions. *Why didn't you protect me? Why was I left alone with him?* Questions she's not ready to ask.

We talk about her grandfather's funeral. She is unable to express the rage her body feels. Her strong, Christian instincts rule, and she mumbles about forgiveness and hoping he's found a degree of peace.

(When my father died, I experienced an exhilarating sense of freedom—"Ding dong, the witch is dead." But to some in my family, his death left them feeling he'd escaped. It had been too easy: a massive heart attack killed him instantly while he was watching a hockey game. I didn't go to his funeral; I've never been to his grave.)

This interview has been difficult for the tough-looking welfare recipient, one of the many Ontario's government has targeted for expecting too much, producing too little. She has enough to cope with without reaching for these feelings. She too lives in a state of disaster preparedness.

Toni tells me about the month when she ran out of toilet paper a good ten days before her cheque was due. How, in frustration and anger at herself, she sat down with pen and paper and roughed out some calculations to prevent a recurrence. I ask her to write it out for me again, fascinated with our different approaches to the same situation:

Toilet Paper
8 rolls: $2.89 every two months, plus tax
280 sheets per roll
280 x 8 = 2,240
3 wasted sheets per roll (stick to the cardboard)
3 x 8 rolls = 24 wasted sheets
2,240 − 24 = 2,216
3 sheets per use x 8 times per day = 24 sheets a day
24 x 61 days = 1,464 sheets
Total available sheets every two months = 2,216
Total use every two months = 1,464
Leaving 752 sheets, or 12 extra sheets per day plus 20 extra.

Now, life's never that simple. The medication she's on causes frequent diarrhea. And she has to also take a diuretic, which means even more frequent peeing. She never just passes by a public toilet.

She throws in an extra calculation she's done.

Maxi Pads
$2.69 each month, plus tax
18 pads per package
Use 4 per day, and 2 extra
Period can only last four days.

I have also run out of toilet paper. Just another one of poverty's indignities, to which I have no response. I've got to admire her grit.

We hear a lot lately about victims' rights. As long as the victim has been murdered, and there's a family to demand justice, we respond to their grief and agony quite well as a society. We know who to target for blame.

Unless, of course, the victim is not killed. Unless, of course, the victim survives, and must for a time go on public assistance, and the perpetrator is never confronted with his crime. Then we as a society get all muddled up, and we start feeling victimized, we start voting for parties like the "neo-conservatives," who appeal to us as "victims"—people being taken advantage of.

LOCAL TELEPHONE RATES NOT A CAUSE OF POVERTY, AGT SAYS

Hull—Low-income Canadians struggling to pay the rising cost of basic phone service should not blame the big telephone companies but instead scold the federal government for the state of the country's social fabric, says an executive with AGT Ltd.

"Local telephone rates are not the cause of poverty," Bohdan Romaniuk told a CRTC hearing yesterday. "If there are households that are giving up other essential goods or services in order to purchase basic telephone service, the problem clearly is not that local service is priced too high....

"This fact points to a much more significant problem in the Canadian social fabric that only government can address. No single industry, representing just a small fraction of consumer expenditures, can ever hope to address such a problem."

...[He] also told members of the Canadian Radio-television and Telecommunications Commission that poor Canadians wouldn't really benefit from a reduction in the cost of local phone service.

That's because the monthly bill for basic phone service represents such a tiny portion of a typical person's overall expenses, he said. A rate cut, [he] contended, would barely be noticed.

(Scott Feschuk, *Globe and Mail*, May 29, 1996)

Toni, when talking about trying to survive on welfare, keeps shaking her head in disbelief.

"He said he wouldn't hurt the disabled."

He being Harris, *he* being the social services minister. Both might as well come from a different planet.

"Do you get angry?"

"Not a lot. Sometimes I think I save it up. I remember, they were endangering my housing. The welfare people. They cut me off, they'd decided I was still eligible for UIC, though I knew I wasn't. I had no money, couldn't pay rent for two months. Forms weren't moving between the right offices, or something. You have to keep right on top of them, and when you don't have a phone, and you can't afford the bus or the subway, there's no way, you know?

"I went a little crazy. About 3:00 a.m., I took this baseball bat and started walking, miles, I was going to do the building in. I was so mad. So frustrated. I'm very lucky I didn't run into any cops—here's me coming up on the welfare office, right down the middle of the street, waving my bat. But the walk helped, you know? I said to myself, 'What the hell are you doing?'"

(I used to take it personally too. When UIC cheques were stalled and stalled and stalled, I figured it was deliberate, a policy of deterrence, a kind of "keep 'em sweating" attitude. It was too stupid and mean to be simple incompetence.)

"Not long after, I found an eviction notice pasted on my freshly painted door. It took forever to get it off. There's still this square of grunge on the wood."

She went to legal aid, went to court, and won. She's still in the same place, but she can't forget how close she came. It seems there's always a little lower you can go, a little more horror just around the corner.

Still, she's made herself a life in Toronto, she has friends living in her building and elsewhere; she's open and friendly and determined to have her say.

"You can use my real name if you want. I know that's important, for credibility, and I don't mind."

For people who have felt powerless and at the mercy of forces that are faceless, the opportunity to tell the truth is deeply meaningful. For people like Toni. For all the people who've spoken to me. It's a refusal to be victimized any more, a refusal to be reduced to a negative cliché.

Whatever the cost.

 castle looms over the top of my street, Casa Loma, lending a feudal air appropriate to the times. A private home built by Sir Henry Pellatt just before World War I, it comes complete with underground stables and a secret staircase. Ten years later, Sir Henry lost his castle to the taxman; he died a pauper.

To get downtown, I walk east on Bloor Street, which starts to get very tony around Avenue Road. I like to create my own mythology or symbolism about the structures and the individuals who people the streets I walk along. For instance, there is a small parkette tucked between the Ontario Institute for Studies in Education and the University of Toronto's Faculty of Social Work. It used to be fronted by a low wall, and the only people who seemed to use the scattering of benches were a group of folks, six at the most, usually only two or three, who were addicted to solvent sniffing. Admittedly not an attractive addition to the neighbourhood, but I kind of liked them being up the nose of social workers and academics.

One afternoon, as I was heading down to the Gerstein Centre to lunch with my friend Paul—maybe a year or so ago —I spotted a clump of official-looking people standing ceremoniously in front of the thigh-high wall, one of whom was holding a sledgehammer.

You might have seen a movie, a true story, about a ghetto-dwelling woman in the States who knocked down a high wall that sheltered dealers and hookers and other nasties, effectively reclaiming the neighbourhood. I figured these folks had seen it too and gotten carried away. Now, none of this may be in fact what was going on, but I like my version.

A big guy in a suit swung the hammer like a golf club, and it made a satisfying thump. Next time I went that way, the wall was gone, and so were the handful of men and women who'd rested there. I was disturbed; there wasn't any dealing or corruption of children happening there, just some people who'd given up struggling. I was glad when they came back and resumed sitting on the benches.

But the fat lady hadn't sung. Not by a long shot.

Next to come were the landscapers, putting in quite pretty borders of flowers and grasses that swayed in the slightest breeze. That didn't stop anybody, either. They stayed like weeds invading a flowerbed, wads of wet paper stuck under their noses.

The latest additions are large, shallow, concrete bowls holding plants, strategically positioned to make entry to the parkette difficult. Nevertheless, I counted eight street people yesterday, having a high old time.

Further down on Bloor is a new cigar store, Holt Renfrew (which still has a doorman for its clientèle), The Irish Shop, The Gap, and at the corner of Bloor and Yonge an ageing plaque proclaiming that all this abundance rests atop land that was once a Potter's Field. The irony is almost as delicious as the fact that the provincial legislature is built over the grounds of a lunatic asylum.

--.--.--

It's difficult, though not impossible, to pace in my room.

From the edge of my futon to the slightly-larger-than-bar fridge is about four paces or six steps, and on a slight diagonal I can do eight paces or ten steps from the door to the radiator. Winter is hell, but in the summer I get outside and walk as often as possible.

I've already done eleven kilometres through the city this afternoon, in my cowboy boots, and I'm starting to feel the threat of erupting blisters.

I am to meet a lady I have only spoken to once on the phone. She is currently housed in a church project after being evicted from her apartment. She told me she'd heard about what I was writing from another resident and assured me she had a tale to tell.

I have a token in my pocket, an almost full pack of smokes and a notebook. On my belt, under my shirt, bounces a pedometer a friend had bought for me in Yorkville last year, so I can keep track of my mileage and try to beat my personal best.

This is a neighbourhood where the poverty is palpable, the streets, the houses, the air filled with dirt and dust and defeat. Seems like apartment ads here should come with a rider: the upwardly mobile need not apply.

−.−.−.−

HARRIS, EVES DINE IN STYLE

It didn't take long for Tory Finance Minister Ernie Eves and Premier Mike Harris to dip into their income tax savings.

After Tuesday's budget announcement, they went for a celebratory dinner....

The restaurant, north of Eglinton Ave., was filled to its 330-seat capacity with six-figure broker types who applauded when the Harris party entered at 9:00 p.m., trailed by three security men.

Eves and Harris ate steak, medium rare, and drank an unpretentious (by Centro standards) bottle of Italian red wine.

At Centro, the tariff for a party of four, with one bottle of wine, is usually about $400.

(Toronto Star, May 9, 1996)

−.−.−.−

We are wary of each other. She meets me at the front door and leads me into the residents' lounge, where the television is on and a pot of coffee brews. She is attractive, in an artsy way, slender, mid-fifties, with an eastern European accent. She wears a loose pullover and black tights, and tucks her legs under her when she sits on the couch kitty-corner from me. I have no idea where or if to start, and our eyes are drawn to the TV screen as if for assistance.

She begins, earning my instant gratitude, by asking questions, easy questions, about my project. I tell her what I can, keeping my natural curiosity in check, but she likes to talk, and soon she's sketching some of her story for me. I leave my notebook closed—note-taking seems inappropriate, or clinical, or something.

When she feels safe, and I have passed whatever test she's set for me, she invites me upstairs to her apartment, where she can tell me things outside the possible overhearing of staff.

She'd told me on the phone that she was once a millionaire.

I caution myself to suspend critical judgment for the time being; I have an irritating tendency towards disbelief, and it's unfair to go into interviews scepticism first. People shouldn't have to prove themselves to be heard. But it seems we both recognize it's there, this need to prove a story in order to be really believed.

When I worked at a drop-in for psychiatric survivors and street people, I met many a twenty-year-old who had served in Vietnam, or written all the Beatles' songs, or been raised by bears. On the other hand, as I often said in my speeches to workers in the mental health system, if I ever got sick again and found myself on a psychiatric ward and was foolish enough to mention my book, television appearances or lunch with the Queen ... well, you get my point.

And this isn't, yet, a crazy lady.

She ushers me into her cramped space. Her bohemian air is played out in the style and furnishings she's been able to keep around her. She has that knack I've always lacked and envied, the ability to express oneself through one's immediate surroundings.

Pushed up against two adjoining walls, a sectional couch sprawls, attractive and comfortable. I am directed to a black leather easy chair, behind which is a pretty, spacious white bird cage housing three annoyed budgies.

On one wall, four arching mirrors, clearly meant for a bigger space, but still working well. The coffee table in front of me holds a lush arrangement of white silk roses. I don't wish to be too obvious in my taking in of her taste and circumstances, so I keep my eyes on hers as she takes a seat on the couch opposite me.

She explained to me downstairs that after her eviction, she'd spent five weeks in a women's shelter, a trial by fire, by total immersion. Clearly, she has a theatrical consciousness of her life, of its ups and downs—a movie in the making, "The Extraordinary Life of...." It comes out in expansive gestures, in almost musical tones and pauses.

Perhaps that has helped to keep her going, got her through the initial devastation to the precariousness of today. Our meeting has taken on somewhat of a conspiratorial air. Or perhaps it's just the intimacy of two women who have been placed in circumstances at least one of them never expected to meet. I can't help nodding as she talks, in recognition of the validity of the points, the observations she makes. What I too have seen and fought against, and often despaired of changing.

She is still struck by the thinness of the line between the haves and have-nots, the breathtaking, backbreaking speed with which one can be impelled to the other side of that line. And the barricades that are constructed, often by the designated helpers, to prevent a going back. I too have lost my breath and bearings: one moment here, the next there, hardly a heartbeat in between. The difference is, I suppose, I knew the terrain; for her, everything is new and nightmarish.

She gets up from the couch, rummages purposefully through her papers, though there has been no specific challenge to the beginnings of her story. As she looks, she draws my attention to a large poster of Ginger Rogers and, more specifically, to a black-inked autograph made out to her.

I can't help it: immediately the jaded part of my mind informs me that anyone can write on a poster. (I visualize punting my brain over distant goal posts.)

She retrieves two items: a thick anniversary report from an established major charity, about the size of two high school yearbooks; and a picture of Ginger (the crowd roars) signing the very same poster as a very glamorous-looking lady (my lady) leans smiling towards her, looking starstruck and at the same time more of a Hollywood figure than the actress she admires.

This is not a woman who could have predicted homelessness for herself at the age of fifty-five, or hunger, or the corrosive effects of dependency on a system that seems to resent any remnants of pride or "obstinacy" or expectation.

She flips through the hardcover charitable report to a back

page labelled "Life Patrons," featuring portraits of the generous; hers is first and prominent. Another practised flip, and we are staring at a young man in a wheelchair about to take a basketball shot; her name is painted on the wheel. With a gesture of "enough said," she closes the book, closes that part of her life, and takes her seat again on the couch.

I'm impressed with the efficiency of her display, and more especially with the lack of maudlin regret. She'd been married to an extremely wealthy man, who she unfortunately trusted and counted on. I don't ask if she loved him, but I suspect she did. He'd always kept his money as his own, though he liked buying her things, like status from charitable giving. When he divorced her, he cut her out of his life, and when he died shortly after, she learned that he'd also cut her out of his will. She was left with an income-producing apartment building and the vulnerability of a woman used to being cared for.

The story of how she was conned out of that building, by a fellow so successful with his numerous shady dealings that he was exposed on "The Fifth Estate," belongs elsewhere; suffice it to say she was ripe for the plucking. And one day she came home, and the locks on her door were changed, and she couldn't get inside.

Most of us believe there is a safety net out there; we need to believe it in order to sleep at night. And any evidence to the contrary, such as the increasing numbers of homeless on the streets, we tend to file under lifestyle choices rather than system failure. She turned to the system she believed in for help. And got it, though it was not what she expected.

She made an appointment with her landlord that day. It was raining so she prepared herself with a rain hat, coat and umbrella and, more important, a positive attitude. They would work it out. Things started to go wrong right away. Buses crawled along in heavy traffic and she arrived fifteen minutes late. The only man at the office claimed to be the property manager; he said that the landlord had another appointment to keep and couldn't wait. She suspected he was the landlord, avoiding possible confrontation and responsibility. He told her the landlord had decided to have the locks changed on her door.

"I didn't believe him. I thought, you know, they had to give you notice."

She was carrying with her all the money she had left, $100, but when the "manager" asked her if she had any money to pay down, caution won out and she shook her head.

"I went back home, still feeling a bit optimistic, put my key in the lock and it wouldn't turn. I tell you, Pat, it was like the whole city fell on my head. I just stood there, in shock. It was November 8, cold. I had $100. And nowhere to go. No toothbrush, no nightgown, nothing. When I could move again, I went up Queen Street, to a place I had always noticed when passing by: the Spadina Hotel. I thought it would be pretty inexpensive, but when I got there, I couldn't believe how awful it was. I'd rather have stayed on the street. I finally ended up at the Executive Motor Inn: it cost $70.

"That night ... thank God I'm not a suicidal person, that I still had so much desire to make it, to survive. I was worried sick about my birds. I spent time looking up numbers and addresses, and the next morning took myself to welfare and asked for emergency assistance. They sent me to a shelter. The staff there gave me a basic change of clothes, a toothbrush, towel and soap. Helped me phone legal aid, but they couldn't help, because the place wasn't covered under the Landlord Tenant Act. It was a commercial property. In the next weeks I negotiated to get my birds taken care of, and to have my furniture picked up and stored."

She spent five weeks in the women's shelter. She isn't over that yet, what she saw, how she felt. Shudders run along her body, visible through the woollen sweater. It's the same reaction I had when I took up tenancy in my psychiatric boarding home, accompanied by the same feeling of shame for that reaction. Downstairs she'd told me:

"I don't want to judge those who drink too much. God knows I understand what drives them to it. Or drugs, for that matter. It's not what I do, but I'm not going to look down my nose at those who do."

But she didn't anticipate having to share the same toilets, the same showers, as street hookers and intravenous users, who had God knows what diseases.

"I've always taken care of myself, you see. Sometimes I think that's the only reason I've survived all this—always careful of my diet, almost a vegetarian, really."

She shows me pamphlets she's picked up for some people living with AIDS who are housed near to her. They came from a health food store and emphasize nutrition and healing, a holistic approach to life and wellness. She once used her diet to control the arthritis she suffers from, but of course that's gone by the board now. The government would rather buy her pills than food, she says with a slightly disgusted shake of her head.

"You know, it's impossible to get fresh food. The food banks have only canned and packaged goods, if you can afford to get to them, if you can carry what they give you. There is a shelter component to this project, and they give meals out to homeless men, women and children at different times on different days. I tried to ask here...." She trails off, clearly troubled.

"What happened?" I ask.

"You understand, I am on welfare. After I pay my rent here, I must pay the storage for what I was able to rescue from my apartment, from my life. It's all I have. Anyway, when that's paid for, I have fifty dollars left for the month. For everything in the month. Imagine.

"Sometimes I eat at the shelter, so I like to help out with the serving, pay back a little. It's something to do. One afternoon, I'm headed over there, and I see this delivery truck backing up. There's all kinds of lettuce, tomatoes, even oranges and carrots. I have a juicer, you see."

She waves vaguely to the alcove where there is a tiny kitchen area. I bite my lip to keep from smiling: a juicer is better evidence than the charity book. We had a running joke at the drop-in about a public health nutritionist we'd brought in to talk to interested members, who we swore said: "First you take your Cuisinart ..."

"It was packed. The truck. So I went in the kitchen and asked the cook if I could take a few things back to my room. He said I'd have to ask the staff. I looked until I found one, and he sighed and told me to show the cook before I left with anything. I took a head of lettuce, some carrots, two tomatoes. The cook said, like he was surprised, 'Is that all you wanted?'"

A brief, triumphant look passes over her face, replaced by a flush of anger.

"But the very next day, under my door, and I found out under everyone's door, comes this memo. Mind you, my name is not mentioned, but I know, and it's so humiliating! 'Residents are not to bother the cooks with requests for food.'

"Pat, you cannot imagine how angry I was. But I thought, I will not take this lying down. We are not talking about champagne and cigars here, we are talking about food. Food! So I write to the head of the organization. A minister, or priest. He doesn't work here, this is just one of the places they run, with people's donations, you see, people who think their money goes where it's needed. I write about my eviction, my welfare cheque, storage, fifty dollars and the memo. I ask to meet with him.

"I get no answer from him. It seems he delegated the supervisor here to answer my letter. After all, why should an important man like him waste time talking to me?"

I'm at the edge of my seat. I still haven't opened my notebook, but I have no fear of forgetting.

"The supervisor writes me this ... letter. It's not long, just enough to say, go to the food bank, and sell off what you have in storage. So simple, really."

I wince, recognizing the staff member's injured righteousness behind the proffered solution. You're not supposed to complain, certainly not supposed to hold out your hand and say, "Please sir, can I have some more...?" If you're used to more, get used to less. Beggars can't be choosers.

We wind the interview down. It's time for me to go while I can still walk without pain from blisters. At least I hope I can.

We ride down together in the small elevator, and I tell her honestly that I admire her courage. Though she doesn't voice it, I see determination and almost hear:

"You ain't seen nothing yet!"

 woman who did all the right things in her marriage. Stayed faithful, raised her children and went out to work, cooked meals and ironed shirts, made love regularly with her husband, contributed to joint accounts and RRSPs, started to plan out their retirement. And her husband comes home one night and tells her he's leaving, he's been having an affair with a younger woman, she makes him feel alive for the first time in years, he's getting out, he's starting over.

All a lie. I've been a fool, living out a lie. Why me? Why my marriage? I don't want to end up a cliché. I don't want to be piled on a mound of statistics.

An often inarticulate, unfocused rage rampages through her thoughts, her life, undoing everything, changing everything that was once permanent.

Not my husband. Not my life.

And she becomes an object of pity, of endless, merciless gossip. "Did you hear about...?"

"It's about time she found out. It's been going on for years."

Or a parent. Distantly aware of the plight of leukemia victims who received bad blood. Who gets a letter one morning informing him that the operation his child had five years ago puts her at possible risk of contamination from blood donations.

Or a senior, who's worked and planned and saved and now looks forward to a well-cushioned old age in a house that's paid for, with an independence that's treasured, who catches his grown children watching him with concern, who overhears conversations: *What if he falls? He's forgetting so much, it could be dangerous. Should he really be driving?*

Every time they visit these days, they bring brightly coloured nursing home pamphlets, keep saying, "You have to be realistic ..."

Those moments. Those life-altering, life-shattering moments. That instantaneous, permanent reduction from all you were to the little you are perceived to be.

Frail elderly. Downsized. Divorced. Victim. Shunted aside. No longer one of us. A burden.

Remember the Lattimer case? The father who bundled up his severely handicapped daughter, *for her sake*, placed her in his truck, *for her sake*, ran the engine, *for her sake*, till she was dead?

The morning after the charges against Lattimer broke on the news, I stood outside the temporary offices of the Ontario Advocacy Commission, trying to understand why I felt so threatened. Joanne, in the advanced stages of MS, one arm still under her control, Tony, with AIDS, Kerry, blind and deaf—we huddled together as though we'd been abandoned on an ice floe, shivering and frightened.

I remember reading a Jewish writer who said that sometimes, in the comfort of a friend's house, or in a bar, he would look around at his companions and wonder, *Who would hide me?*

We wonder, who would value us? As the debate around the Lattimer case raged, I grew to fear what friends would say, if their sympathy would be with the father, how they would react. I didn't want to know.

It was a bitterly cold time.

No one wants Lattimer to hang, to spend what remains of his life in prison. At least, I don't. But somewhere, the wrongness of what he did should be very clearly, unequivocally, brought into every home, every heart.

It was foreshadowing; those of us who have already been marginalized should be grateful that we've had a head start on the realities of our "brave new world." More time to process the consequences of dependence, of difference, of inconvenience.

—.—.—

We've all heard about or experienced the corporate decision to downsize. How workers first hear the rumours of layoffs and firings. How everyone walks on tiptoes, waiting, praying they will not be affected. How abruptly tenuous and fragile a previously stable, comfortable life becomes.

Every time the bosses are called into a meeting, the workers think: *this is it,* and steel themselves for the announcement.

And when the announcement is made, and security guards start showing up at people's desks, waiting none too patiently for the now former employee to gather up any personal possessions, and escort him or her to the front door, those who've survived this round look for all the reasons why these employees were targeted. Look for a less arbitrary pattern, in order to feel safer.

He never worked as hard as me. Wouldn't be available for overtime. His department wasn't producing.

And those left in their jobs try not to wonder what will happen to those who've lost them. But sometimes that's hard, when you know more about their lives than is comfortable right now. When you know one of the fired is over fifty, that his wife has been sick, that he was already having trouble making ends meet.

The last count I heard was a million and a half unemployed across the country. A million and a half walking wounded.

–·–·–

ONTARIO, MICHIGAN WELFARE STANDARDS SHOW BOLD CONTRAST
As the province considers workfare, U.S. assistance conditions are already far stricter

Toronto—Michigan is poised to make mothers of babies older than six weeks return to work or lose their benefits [they now have six months]....

In Michigan, a single mother with two children receives $459 (U.S.) a month to cover rent, clothing, transportation and most of the family's food [there is also a small food-stamp subsidy]....

In Ontario, a single mother of one child receives $977 (Cdn) a month, down from $1,221 before the Ontario government cut welfare rates by 22 percent on Oct. 1. A single person receives $520 a month, down from $663, and a couple with two children receives $1,202, down from $1,503.

(Jane Gadd, *Globe and Mail*, November 4, 1995)

Earlier, my existence would have confirmed your world view. Someone who "pulled herself up by her bootstraps." I have all these plaques and certificates on my wall, even a medal hanging under my hat. Outstanding public service. Outstanding character and achievement. Outstanding contribution and achievement. Even, somewhere, a congratulatory letter from you, as leader of the third party. Even, somewhere, a letter from Mulroney.

Now I know it's the flip side of that world view my life would confirm—too lazy to work, too dependent on the public purse, a social pariah who won't get off the wagon to help push.

-.-.-

She whispers, and at the same time apologizes for whispering.

Her name is Joanna, and she's calling from the place where she works as a volunteer. They don't know, there, that she's on welfare.

"It's just that, well, you read about it every day, how we're all freeloaders, drug addicts, alcoholics and prostitutes. People are so uninformed, so ignorant."

She wants to help me with this book, wants to tell me her story, though she doesn't feel very important.

"I was downsized, you see. I was with them seven years. I was the marketing co-ordinator, and they were closing our branch. I could have stayed with the parent company, but the only opening was in the mailroom, so I took the buy-out package. It was a gradual shut-down, and I was asked to stay right to the end, which turned out to be right before Christmas."

Originally from Nova Scotia, raised in a middle-class environment, her father was in the armed forces, her mother worked as an interior decorator. She laughs when I ask her what she'd wanted to be when she was younger.

"Like most kids, I wanted to be famous, successful, have lots of money. After I got over that, I thought perhaps teaching, or being a youth worker."

She's a little embarrassed when I ask about university. She went, for a while, but there were so many jobs around in the eighties, so much opportunity to start earning a living. She grew impatient, she quit and went to work.

The office is getting busy around her, and we agree she should call me back after she's put her son to bed that night. When she calls, she's on a borrowed, portable phone, with weak batteries, because she knew she'd be standing outside where the conversation wouldn't upset her eldest. She's apologetic about the bad connection, but we manage.

She continues to tell me about her jobs in Nova Scotia, when working was the same as breathing, really. And work she did, sometimes holding down three jobs at a time, especially after her first son was born. His father wasn't in the picture, so it was up to her. And she was up to the task.

She's clearly proud of herself, how she managed, including taking night courses at university. Even after moving to Toronto, it seemed there were jobs everywhere. Confident, attractive, hard-working and determined—she had the qualities that were valued by employers, and she never worried about making it. Didn't worry about finding another job—not too much, anyway.

Her buy-out, if she was careful, would last her about a year, and she wasn't alone any more; she lived with her self-employed husband.

Her next pregnancy was unexpected, and in retrospect she wonders what the hell she thought she was doing. Her first son was a teenager, and here she was about to have a baby.

He's two now. She and her husband separated shortly after he was born.

"My husband does his best, tries to help. But he hasn't been able to get much work either, and anyway, whatever he contributes is taken off my cheque, dollar for dollar, so you're never really ahead. And now, with the cutbacks, I receive even less."

She has attacked the problem of her unemployment with all the energy she can muster. She's out every day, and she demands access to programs that might help her find her way back to the shrinking work force.

She's fortunate to have a job counsellor who also has a young child, and who seems to empathize: she's become rather a cheerleader, and an advocate. But the welfare office itself frightens Joanna.

"It's got to be the worst place ... everyone's so keyed up. Workers there are afraid of losing their jobs, and they're having to do more than they used to. And the clients—there are people who are on the verge of being evicted, who need help now. And the waiting, and waiting. You can feel the frustration, the anger, the desperation building. And the security guards—there's a big guy that walks around with all these tattoos. I know I'm probably being paranoid, but I'll never bring my children there. I keep thinking someone's going to blow, someone's going to come in with a gun and start shooting everyone. It happens, doesn't it? And if it happens anywhere, it can happen there. You feel it."

To get her son to day-care, she travels on two buses and a subway. She confesses that by the time she drops him off, she already feels as though she's put in a whole day. It's the discouragement, of course, she recognizes that, and the energy it takes to fight it off. But she does, and goes to yet another course that advises people on finding work in the nineties.

She's the only Canadian-born person in this course, everyone else is a recent immigrant. It wasn't described as a course for new Canadians, but that's what it really is, which is why, she thinks, she had to be so persistent to get in.

"You should see the skills these people have! Teachers, electrical engineers, and they can't get work." They root for each other, learn together, share techniques and tactics.

Within the last month, she's had her first job interview in two years. They even called her back for a second interview.

"Everyone in the course was so happy for me, so sure I'd gotten the job. I kept saying, 'I haven't got it yet.'" But, she confesses, it looked so good she'd started to hope.

"Two weeks have gone by. I keep in touch, they tell me they haven't made a final decision yet. But I think they have."

It's so hard these days even to get one interview. So many people are out of work, employers can pick and choose. They certainly don't have to be sensitive about getting back to people.

I ask her how she dealt with this past Christmas.

"Well," this is hard for her, I can tell, "I only paid half my rent in December. It was the only way. Of course, that meant January I had to pay one and a half months' rent, but December is so emotional, you know? So our Christmas was pretty limited. It's not so much what presents I couldn't buy. Even when I had money I wouldn't go buying expensive things. That's not what Christmas should be about. But I live near the Dufferin Mall, and each year there's this Sally Ann tree, and my oldest and I would go and pick a name and donate a wrapped gift.... And, of course, you try to invite someone over who doesn't have much, at least for Christmas dinner. Try to do your bit. That's Christmas."

She was raised a Catholic, but she doesn't go to church much any more.

"I don't feel I need to prove my spirituality. I try to be

honest, kind, compassionate, healthy. We say our prayers and sometimes we read the Bible."

These are the values she tries hard to instil in her children.

I go back to her very recent disappointment.

"Maybe there's another way of looking at it," I suggest. "You know how many people apply for a job like that, especially with that company, and you're one of the few people they noticed enough to give you an interview. And then, they were so impressed they called you back. That's what you should be dwelling on, because, after two years of looking, when you got a chance, you shone. That's gotta bode well for the future, don't you think?"

I hear her smiling now through the phone, bad connection and all. "Could be. To tell you the truth, I was very discouraged. I was so close. Then nothing. But of course you're right, that's the way to see it. Happened once, it'll happen again. Maybe all the way next time!"

I promise to get back to her in a week or so, after I type up our conversation. I don't tell her how much I wish I had a magic wand.

-.-.-

There was a spider on the wall in my bathroom this morning, a small, ugly spider. I will make the effort to trap flies and beetles and let them go outside, since, even if they were so inclined, they couldn't bite. Not these guys, though. I spent a moment puzzling how to do him in, then grabbed my can of deodorant spray in my own version of chemical warfare. Of course, immediately after, I was struck by the waste, not just of the tiny embodiment of malevolent life, but also the three or four days' worth of deodorant I'd coated him with.

I'm thinking back to my conversation with Joanna, and how animated her voice got when she was speaking of the work she used to do. Her remembered value. She knew from the courses she'd fought her way into that these days you had to reinvent yourself. And she was trying, taking her previous job experience in marketing to companies working in environmentally friendly products and recycling.

"I introduced recycling in my office, then got together with the building manager to get every floor involved. I probably drove people crazy, telling them to use both sides when they made copies, reminding them to put waste paper into that box." She'd giggled, remembering.

It does feel good, for a few moments, but the price is high; you're brought back very abruptly to your present reality, and the pain is fresh and sharp and new all over again.

—.—.·.—

Annette and I agree to meet in front of A-way Express, on Broadview Ave. She has a pretty face, and, by an extraordinary act of will, eyes that shine through the medication fog that is the condition of her existence.

I invite her to accompany me to a neighbouring coffee shop, where I can smoke, and I have one bad moment when I learn the cost of two ordinary coffees comes to $2.40. There was a time when I wouldn't have noticed, or particularly cared, but that time is long gone. It's going to be another long walk home. Not surprisingly, I grouse to myself, we are almost the only customers here.

She is nervous, as though I'm a policeman about to give her the third degree. Her movements are stiff, her hands do a reassuring, repetitive check: from her jacket to the pouch around her waist, back to her jacket, to the pouch. Translation: *I'm okay, I'm solid, I'm here, I can do this.*

I spend a few moments going through what I'm about, what I'm doing with this book. She nods stiffly, clearly steeling herself.

"Want to tell me a bit about your parents? What growing up was like?"

I learn she grew up as an army brat, frequent moves punctuating and defining her childhood. Her father drank too much, slept around too much, and as soon as the kids were grown, her mother divorced him. Annette decided to enter the army herself, as soon as she was old enough, and over the next four years she enjoyed her service.

She smiles, lightening the tension straining her face.

"My mother taught me to cook, and the army taught me to cook for five hundred."

She married an army man, and after becoming pregnant, made the decision to quit.

Almost predictably, in those patterns that we fail to recognize till it's too late, her husband drank too much and was often verbally abusive. When he was transferred overseas, she and her baby girl stayed behind, and the painful process of divorcing him was begun. She took a computer inputting job, placing her daughter in day-care, determined to rebuild her life. Then her baby was diagnosed with leukemia. Stress mounted: her terror for her child, trying to juggle endless hospital appointments and her work, trying to stretch her income to pay the rising tide of bills.

"I started to get sick." She says this with palpable undertones of personal failure.

How did that sickness manifest itself?

She describes a gradual, insidious, escalating paranoia. It was masked in apparent reasonableness—she didn't just wake up one morning with certifiable thoughts that might have warned her she was suffering from a mental illness.

"I don't remember a lot from that time. Things are still confused in my mind. I do remember being afraid that people were whispering about me, or I thought they were. I also thought the people in my office were trying to get me fired. And my mother. I'd moved back home, and even there, nothing seemed right."

At no point could she clear her head enough to gain any perspective on what was happening to her. It's not as though she could talk about it, trust enough to talk to the very people she was so suspicious of. How could she believe anything they told her? She just tried to hang on, get through the days, through the whispers and the looks and the growing fear.

And then, of course, at least one of the fears came true, when her supervisor told her she was fired.

"I wouldn't leave my computer, wouldn't look up from the keyboard. It was like, if I kept working, they couldn't really let me go, you know? Soon, it seemed like the whole office was gathered around my desk, trying to get me to leave. They even called my mother. Then they physically pulled me away, almost tore me away.

"And that was that. I went to the day-care to pick up my child, and my mother was waiting there. She said I really had to go to the hospital, that I needed help. For my safety, and for the safety of my child. I didn't believe her, but I had no choice: I went, stayed for three days. I wouldn't take medication—after all, I wasn't sick—and they let me go.

"That was the first time. The second time, the police came and got me. I spent a month in hospital then."

She shivers a little, then looks me straight in the eye and makes a courageous confession.

"I'd hit my mother."

Because she was so ashamed and frightened by her violent outburst, this time she took the meds. In a month they felt she was sufficiently stabilized, that the incident had been stress related, episodic in nature and not likely to be repeated. Her meds were discontinued.

It wasn't till the third hospitalization that she was finally diagnosed with schizophrenia. And she made a very difficult, but to her very necessary, decision to stay on meds the rest of her life.

She had to endure a two-year custody battle with her ex-husband, who had remarried and wanted his child back. He of course invoked her illness as proof of her inability to parent her child. It seemed sometimes that her life was now just a series of battles. But she beat him in court and kept her daughter, who's now twelve, and in remission.

Although she gets income from various places—child support, a small army pension, child tax benefits—everything comes off (dollar for dollar) from her welfare cheque, leaving her with nothing more than the usual amount.

I ask her to run through her income and expenses for me:

Income: $820 a month (without A-way salary)

Expenses:

Rent: $433
Utilities: $200 (heat, electricity, cable, phone)
Metropass: $65 (A-way received a grant to subsidize
                passes)
Groceries: $320
Child care: $20 (was $1 a weekday, now $7.70 a day)

Total: $1,038

In a good month, she can earn $200 from her work at A-way (though everything over $160 comes off her welfare cheque); she's never earned more, and usually it's less. Even in the best-case scenario, she's still in the hole.

"Tell me how you manage on that."

She's relaxing a bit more now, and flashes a smile.

"A very strict budget, of course. And a lot of common sense. Bi-way instead of the Bay. Always keeping your eye open for specials. But I'm very fortunate. I have my mother, who's very supportive. I live in the basement apartment of her house, and we share the costs of hydro and telephone. And I have a fiancé." She is proud and blushing at the same time.

"He's also a survivor, he has depression. He doesn't take medication, he wants to manage without it. He has a job. He doesn't earn very much, but he goes to work every day."

It was harder before. She felt much more isolated. Worried

all the time about money, her stomach constantly in knots.

"I couldn't go out, there was nowhere to go, and even if there was someplace, I couldn't afford to get there. Nowhere to meet people, to try and relax. I feel so bad for those without the emotional supports I have, without family and friends. I remember, my daughter would want to go to a movie, and I had to send her alone, because I couldn't afford to pay for both of us. Now we go with my fiancé. My daughter really likes him, she almost won't go any more if it's just us two."

Her daughter's at that age where clothing is really important: style, make.

"How do you handle not being able to afford the kinds of things she wants? Do you talk to her about your budget restrictions?"

"I let her pick out her own clothes, and I'll tell her if things are too expensive. You have to take a firm hand sometimes. She'll fuss and fume occasionally when I have to say no, but I believe she understands I don't do it just to be mean. I give her two dollars a week allowance, but she has to have her household chores done, she has to earn it, you know?"

Annette is reasonably—some may think unreasonably—content with her life. She loves her mom, her daughter, and her fiancé; she loves her job and the acceptance she's found. She probably has no idea what a triumph her life is.

oday is the first anniversary of the Harris government's election to public office. Only one year ago; so much damage and destruction in only twelve months.

I don't go to many demonstrations any more, not for some years. In Montreal, they used to be an adventure, what with the riot police and the Trotskyites always setting each other off, catching everyone else in between. I used to try and melt away as soon as the first paddy wagons were being rocked, ditching the anti-war placard, assuming a disinterested air while checking out doorways to duck into. I knew what it felt like to be mowed down by police motorcycles and whacked by their batons (clubs, really). Just for being there, being in the way.

Toronto demos always struck me as overly polite. When the

Ku Klux Klan were hounded out of Parkdale and reappeared in the east end, I was part of the crowd that watched in disbelief as idiot thugs in white sheets and hoods stood on the balcony of the house they'd rented, feeling nauseated that a woman, with White Power tattooed across her chest, stood among them giving demonstrators the finger. No question: in Montreal, they would have been swarmed and disrobed. In Toronto, everyone kept a polite, though noisy, distance.

Our community participated in "Timbrell-town," during the province's last Conservative regime, a tent-city set up in Queen's Park to draw attention to the need for subsidized housing, named for the Conservative minister of health, Dennis Timbrell. And I've made short, punchy speeches from the podium on the stairs of the Legislature, along with a loose coalition of anti-poverty activists and Opposition members. So I must have been in a bad mood the day I examined the faces of young men and women heading out towards a march called for something or other—when marching was still a safe, civilized way to spend an afternoon—and saw in them a ridiculous self-importance, determination and, worst of all, accomplishment.

Never again, I muttered to myself.

But here I am, on my way to this demo and working through two decisions I have to make before leaving my room. *NOW* magazine, the only paper I can afford on a regular basis (it's free), has a notice that the demo will be starting at Yonge and Rosedale, in the park opposite the subway. Do I use up one of my last two tokens, or walk there? I know I'll be spending most of the day on my feet, I don't want to be blistered before I start. It's definitely a cowboy boot day, cool and overcast. I can easily walk home from Queen's Park, where everyone will end up, so okay, I decide, I'll subway.

I can afford one meal today. Now? Or later? I dither. Ordinarily, I'd be drinking lots of water to deal with hunger pangs until I can eat, but that's out. I can't see the current crop of security and police letting people use the bathrooms in the Legislature. I decide to wait. I hate going to bed hungry, it's impossible to sleep.

I wear a short-sleeved shirt in case the weather clears up, and my black leather jacket in case it doesn't. And my fall/winter hat, which is much cooler (in the sixties sense of the word) than my summer hat. I also carry my umbrella.

I'm more apprehensive than usual as I sit on the train; there's been a lot of overreaction on the part of police at Queen's Park just lately, a lot of enthusiastic bashing and clubbing seems to go on. But I feel a need to be with others on this day, to confirm in my own head that there are others who feel as I do. Harris's approval rating is consistently high, and over the past year I've found myself nervously watching my neighbours for signs of covert hostility: Which of you is doing this? Which of you is cheerleading? Why do you hate us so much?

It reminds me of the time I got so spectacularly lost, trying to find an upscale address where a Canadian Mental Health Association annual meeting was to be held. I was employed at PARC at the time, so I had, you know, more of a sense of legitimacy, but it didn't help at all where I was.

In a grey fedora, a different black leather jacket and jeans, I found myself in the strangest neighbourhood. The Bridle Path? What the hell kind of name is that for a street, anyway? Like a nervous white couple making a series of wrong turns and winding up in Harlem, I had walked my way into what felt like a really bad place for someone like me. I was waiting for the blood-curdling sounds of dogs baying in pursuit. I heard 911 calls being made from the recessed mansions. I just wanted to get out of there. Sweat dropping into my eyes, I picked up the pace: *C'mon, c'mon, get moving, hurry up before you're seen.*

Not a bus came along. Not a taxi to hail. It seemed like I walked forever. Vowing never to return.

This outing also begins badly. I'm trailing behind two other attendees and I hear them being told by some kind of march official that the site's had to be changed to Old City Hall.

I blow out a lot of air and get back on the subway. At least they had the sense to make sure we were told before we had to pay another token, which would have scotched any marching I might have done. It makes for good right-wing fodder though: the left is in such a mess it can't even organize a demo properly.

Luckily for my state of mind, by the time I've made my way up the stairs exiting from the Queen Street subway, I can see the edges of what looks to be a good, noisy crowd. Someone is valiantly trying to be heard over the noise—I can make out a woman's voice. This is supposed to have been organized by the National Action Committee on the Status of Women and labour, part of a province-by-province prelude to the big event, a march scheduled for later in the month in Ottawa.

A number of small, Wheel Trans type buses are slowly emptying out, and one older lady who's just liberated herself from the interior of one of them, and whose face contorts spasmodically from tardive dyskinesia, hits me up for a cigarette. She's excited—this is no regular outing to the park—and as I hand her a couple of smokes and light one for her, we talk a bit, having to lean in to each other to hear.

She points out her bus to me, as I nod, and not apropos to much she tells me she's German, came to Canada sixteen years ago. She's awfully pleased with the cigarettes, and when I say goodbye, she catches up to me to shake my hand and tell me her name. We grin at each other, kindred spirits, and I wander around, trying to get a sense of who else is here. I am more comfortable here than in smaller gatherings, or same-sized social events, and I move easily from one pocket to another, each identified by banners held high. I keep bumping into employees from the Gerstein Centre, which is nice, and recognize demo regulars from times past. Police are at the edges of the crowd, but they're smiling and polite and determined to be helpful. The march is getting under way.

You will probably be surprised to know I feel much like you do about the professional defenders of the poor, the seniors, and the disabled. Not for all the same reasons....

Many of the problems of the poor involve too many people receiving too much money to help the poor with their problems.

At the recent hearings into the omnibus bill, agency after agency, union spokespeople, doctors ... all argued that hurting them hurts their clients. These are the only scenarios when clients are trotted out, and appear to be actively listened to.

Instead of being assisted in saying I need a

decent job, people are encouraged to say, "Save my
social worker, save my agency, save my food bank,
save my doctor," who will then, I hope, get around
to the business of saving me.

I'm looking for people who don't usually come out to
events like this, the newly motivated middle class, and I'm
looking too for those with telltale faces: hungry, unhealthy,
impoverished.

What I see around me, flowing or stalled or just coming
together, are: Native groups, women demanding day-care,
union locals, anti-poverty and anti-racism organizations, a
heartening number of men and women in wheelchairs, AIDS
advocates, people working with refugees and new immigrants,
the usual sprinkling of political ideologues flogging their thin
newspapers, seniors, geographical communities, church groups,
legal aid workers holding petitions against laser fingerprinting
of welfare recipients, others drumming up support for victims
of sexual harassment, NDP MPPs.

I pass one hawker of the socialist/people's forum/daily
worker/anarchist monthly who touts: "Find out the real reasons behind the O.J. verdict," giving me my first real laugh of
the day, lightening my mood and, I pretend, the sky.

Every time we pass cameras, I hide my cigarette like we
used to do in high school, imagining the usual censorious
comments: "They can always afford to smoke, though, can't
they."

I would have preferred a more dramatically silent march,
not one punctuated by tired slogans and a funereal pace. I

don't have the energy to shout, and I'm starting to feel chilled as well as damp.

I'm still mentally seeking some resolution to the ambivalence I feel towards NAC, as a woman who's been frequently immersed in poverty and increasingly aware of class and class war. For years now, I have felt that organized feminism fails those most in need by concentrating on middle-class issues, values and causes.

Less ambivalent than angry, I'm disturbed by the large union presence. It seems to me it would have been better if the banners and placards they carried read *Mea Culpa* and accepted some responsibility for enabling Harris to take power, to take away possibilities from the disadvantaged, to steal what heart they had left.

After the speeches from the steps of the Legislature, which of necessity are only a series of slogans, I try to ignore the mounted police off in the distance and resume my wandering, searching for my own version of diversity. I'm chilled down to the bone, trembling a bit from cold and hunger, but I'm glad of the people, the crowds, who, even if they are still the same faces, are believers, who do try to make a difference, who still have enthusiasm, who still fight on, who do make me feel less alone. I cut through the University of Toronto on my way home.

Two weeks later, the only lasting effect for me personally, of course, is lingering fever, sneezing and coughing.

-.-.-

WOMEN SLAM TORY POLICIES
March protests cutbacks

Some 3,500 angry women marched on Queen's Park yesterday to protest social cuts made by Premier Mike Harris during his first year of power.

The noisy crowd chanted anti-Harris slogans as they marched along Queen St. W., from Old City Hall, up University Ave., to the heavily secured Legislature.

The Women's March Against Poverty was protesting government cuts to social programs, unemployment, poverty and the lack of child-care.

(Tom Godfrey, *Toronto Sun*, June 9, 1996)

 recently sat in on a meeting of staff at an aboriginal women's shelter. I was feeling a little offensive in my cowboy hat and Aussie outback coat, but, luckily for me, the director of the shelter had already made her own polit-ically incorrect gaffe, or so she felt, so I was off the hook.

She'd stood outside with me as I smoked a cigarette, and while talking about the cut-backs and their efforts to stay afloat, she'd confessed that she sometimes feels "a little schizoid." I could see her bite her tongue, and I grinned while she apologized, a little flustered, "I don't know why I say things like that."

The women exuded a quiet strength as they listened to me explain what I was writing about, and why, and then we talked a little about the setbacks the shelter itself has experienced under the present government. They've recently lost their staff pension plan, which took them years to get in the first place.

None of these workers are fat cats. They are struggling almost as much as their clients to keep body and soul together, to keep their children fed and clothed. "But it's nothing new. We've lived like this all our lives, it's all too familiar."

The conversation ranged from the increasing cost of peanut butter, now that more people know it's a good meat substitute, to having to ask for subtotals (and enduring the clerk's exasperated look) at grocery stores, all too aware of the little bit of money in your purse, to trying to access mainstream services for clients those services would rather not deal with.

We seem to share, you and I, a paternalistic streak or two. Mine is protective, yours corrective. I do not believe that all who suffer are noble, the same as I do not believe that all those who cause suffering do evil, are evil.

I believe people make choices and should accept the consequences. That includes abused kids who grow into abusers, poor kids who take out their poverty on the property of others, men who batter their fears into the faces of women. It also includes communities that create the circumstances that foster abandonment, neglect, poverty, ignorance and fear.

We all live and die with the choices we've made.

Later on, I stand outside with a woman just released from the crisis unit of a downtown hospital. Her arms are covered with scars, self-inflicted slash marks, and we smoke together while she speaks proudly of her twelve-year-old son's obsession with reading.

"He lives with his father now, goes to school every day. I think maybe he's a genius."

She's on her way to the drugstore with a two-page prescription that she shows me. I can only make out a few of the items the doctor has scrawled: Librium, Haldol, Tylenol 3s. It's a wonder she's able to stand.

"The hospital lost my shoes, so they gave me this pair," she says, liking them, and their apparent sturdiness. She hasn't noticed yet that the sole has come badly unglued in the front and is now flapping open.

I go upstairs, and soon I'm deep in conversation with another woman, who leaves me shaking my head even days later. I find myself wondering what Ms. Wong would make of this woman; I know Mike Duffy at CTV would declare himself totally vindicated.

She had a difficult enough childhood to cause her to run away at age fifteen, preferring life on the street to what awaited her at home. It was inevitable that she'd fall into addiction and prostitution, two years of both.

"I was just lucky that this guy I met could see beneath all that, that he took me in, cleaned me up, gave me a home. Even married me. He made me feel better about myself. He was twice my age, but we were happy together. We had two kids, a good life. He worked every day, brought home his paycheque."

He was killed in a house fire when she was nineteen. Since

then, she has been receiving survivor benefits, and from time to time that's been her only source of income.

We are talking in the crafts room. She's being shown how to make her own dream-catcher by a very gentle man who stays silent most of the afternoon. She shows me with pride the artistically designed cross she's created out of a couple of dozen burnt wooden match sticks. In the centre of the cross she has glued a collection of variously sized and coloured pigeon feathers.

"See what you can do with useless stuff?"

The second man she married wasn't as nice. It seemed as though in the blink of an eye she had four children, a husband who abused her and no kind of life at all. She made the decision to put the children in the care of Catholic Children's Aid and got out.

And married again. Had another child, whom she was determined to keep. The baby girl had cancer, terminal cancer.

She has the hard face that comes with street life and the struggle to survive, but it softens as she speaks of the Children's Wish Foundation. She, her toddler and her husband made a trip to Disneyland.

"You know, they even had a huge white limousine waiting for us at the airport. At least she got to ride in a white limo, about a year and a half before we had to put her into that black one. I made up all these thank-you cards when we got back, pasted her picture on them, her standing with Mickey Mouse, looking so happy."

She lowers her head, pretends to fuss over her nails, which are long and perfectly applied paste-ons. First rule of the streets: don't display weakness, sentimentality.

Her third husband did everything but hit her, eventually throwing her out of their home. She moved to downtown Toronto from the much smaller city that she'd grown up in, to a room opposite Allan Gardens. Of course, she doesn't tell me that she blew her benefit cheque on liquor, just says vaguely that it wasn't enough to meet her expenses and pay her rent.

"I had a dog for a while, you know, a really nice animal. Do you know the park? Well, it's different in the day. Normal, regular people use it, walk their pets, enjoy the sun, that kind of thing. I used to walk my dog there too, and those gentlemen who sell their trade there, they'd come up and pet him, and I'd give them smokes, and maybe buy them coffee sometimes."

I interrupt her monologue with a question: "When you say 'sell their trade,' do you mean they're male prostitutes?"

"Nah, crack dealers. I mean, it's their business, and it doesn't bother me, as long as they don't try to get me on it, y'know? I told them that, I don't care what you do, just don't push it on me. And they didn't. They treated me like I was innocent, like I was someone special."

She lost the dog the day she lost her place. She went to a women's shelter, but things kept deteriorating. She has to keep in touch with the worker at the Catholic Children's Aid, with the lawyer that's trying to get her access to the children, and welfare to try and supplement the survivor benefits that come to less than three hundred dollars a month.

Anyone who's tried to speak to a social worker knows how frustrating it is to try and get through on phone lines, and even when you are connected, you often find yourself on hold for long periods of time while your file is searched for.

"Apparently there was some kind of rule at the shelter that

you could only use the phone for ten minutes at a time. Christ, I'd spent that long just trying to get past the busy signal. I was frustrated and angry and shaking even before they told me I had to get off the line, and they must have been afraid I was going to get violent with them, because all of a sudden I was told I had to leave the place. They said it was because I'd abused the phone, but I'm pretty sure it was because they thought I was going to abuse them. I wasn't. But that didn't matter. I was out, with a list of, God, I don't know, about seventy other shelters I could try."

She couldn't phone them, of course, to find out if they had any beds open for the night, and even if they did she wouldn't have been able to get there. No money for transportation.

"So there I was, for the first time in twenty years, out on the streets, looking at having to be a prostitute again. Eventually, I figured I'd go over to Allan Gardens, where at least I knew some of the people, those guys I told you about, who might give me a hand. They were shocked to see me, it was about one in the morning, they figured something really bad had happened. And they were worried about my dog. They told me, there were about eight of them in the park by then, they'd protect me if I wanted to sleep under one of the picnic tables, they'd sit around it so nobody'd see me cause all their legs would be in the way. I didn't feel like sleeping, I was too worried, you know, so they bought me coffee and some smokes, and we just shot the breeze till 4:30 or so.

"I should'a told you before, but in the building where I'd had my room, there were professional girls living there too, and I got to know some of them, since I was once in the business myself. When things got tight for me, I'd let them use my shampoo and deodorant, I'd French-braid their hair, y'know, so they looked cleaner, more sophisticated, so they could up their price maybe 50 percent. A hairdresser might charge twenty, thirty dollars for that kind of braid, but what we used to do was, I'd arrange to meet them at a doughnut shop on their break, and they'd buy me some food, and cigarettes and stuff.

"So one of the ladies I knew came to the park early that morning for a buy, and she sees me and it just so happens that she has a customer who's really into *ménage à trois*. I just got lucky, you know?"

She has finished winding a leather strip tightly around the metal circular frame and has begun the spider web design that will make up the core of the dream-catcher.

I ask her how it felt to be back hooking.

"You just turn off part of your mind. You gotta think, well, a guy goes out, he buys work boots, and he puts them to work to make money. I put my body to work. It's the same thing, really."

Her friend, whom she describes as having looked out for her, helps her decide on a safe corner for the night to come. Safe from annoyed, territorial pimps, that is.

Her first solo is a retired army sergeant, from out of town. She is quite proud of the fact that he looked around at what was on offer before he chose her.

"He said I was the cleanest-looking lady out there."

He had a motel room and paid seventy dollars for forty-five minutes with her, as well as arranging for her to meet him back there in the morning for "continental breakfast, you know, a couple of rolls and jam," she laughs, while I try to look as though I already knew she wasn't talking about *breakfast* breakfast.

The next guy she describes as "kinky."

"He was a young guy with this spanking-new pick-up truck, I mean, there weren't even ashes in the ashtray. His thing was, he wanted to drive up and down Yonge Street while I was giving him a hand job. It was kind of funny. Anybody looking at us would have thought we were a regular couple, out on the town. Anyway, he paid me fifty bucks. But the last guy was the best, even if he didn't have much money. He was sitting on the curb, offered me twenty bucks just to kind of lap-dance, he didn't even take it out. Easiest twenty I ever made.

"I should'a quit right after him, but I got greedy and went back to my corner. A cute guy pulls over, I get in, and just as we decide on the price, he busts me. Shit. What it was, they see a new face, they move in, I guess. So he writes me a ticket, they don't take you in any more like they used to. He was nice enough, didn't confiscate my earnings, though I guess he could have. I told him I was trying to earn enough to get a place to live, and he was sympathetic. Still gave me the ticket, though."

Her intricate webbing has sagged and collapsed, and we laugh together when she quips: "It doesn't want to be catching my dreams!"

We pause for a bit while she listens carefully to how to make it tighter.

She can't plead guilty, CCAS might find out; it would be a major setback in her efforts to see her kids. Legal aid doesn't cover this kind of charge any more, and the cheapest lawyer she can find wants $150 up front to represent her. So she's still working.

She's on a waiting list for longer-term housing; waiting lists are a fact of life these days.

And she has had some legitimate work, as an extra in Toronto's burgeoning movie business. In the next few days, she's trying out for two bit parts, one as a street person, another as a tired hooker.

She laughs, and plucks at the clean white sweatshirt with the stylized logo across the front that came from the donations box.

"I'll have to dress down, they'll never hire me in these clothes. They want you to look the part."

As I'm packing up, I venture to ask her how she handles any fears she might have about the dangers of getting into strangers' cars.

"Listen, except for my first husband, the men I've known for the last ten years have been a lot more dangerous than any stranger who's picked me up."

'm waiting for Nora at Dooney's. I worked at A-way again today and I'm having some culture shock moving from one identity to another: from down-and-out courier to down-and-out writer.

I remember vividly the day I first met her husband, Joey. It was at the inquest into the death of John Dimun, a PARC member and resident of my former boarding home killed by (among other factors) malnutrition. Joey was sitting behind me and tapped me on the shoulder to whisper, "I've just been reading about you." (He was talking about June Callwood's book on the life and death of Margaret Fraser, *Twelve Weeks in Spring*.) He attended the inquest every day, writing columns that were alternately sharp, incisive, sometimes funny, sometimes despairing.

Soon after, I was invited to supper and met Nora. Nora's son Brennan—Joey's stepson—lives in a Parkdale boarding home, and I was able to persuade Joey to serve on the PARC board, and later Nora agreed to sit on the Gerstein Centre board.

I still believe, after a decade, that they have no idea how foreign their lives are to me.

It's glorious, sitting out on the patio, drinking decaf au lait, resting my very tired feet and watching the passing parade on Bloor Street. I'm trying to frame some questions that are more difficult to formulate, I suspect, than to answer. I want to know how she was able to bridge the classes, and not just able but willing. And why so few in the mid- to upper-middle classes do.

She waves at me, from the extra height provided by the heels she sports today, and with an open smile and an apology for being late takes a seat opposite me. I am fond enough of her that it's difficult to see her objectively, but she carries a sparkling brightness with her, accentuated today by her more formal work outfit.

She's American by birth, raised in a very wealthy suburb of New York. By the time she'd reached the age of majority, she was more than ready to get away, and she left immediately for Canada.

Her grandfather made a lot of money. Nora's mother was raised in a house staffed by butlers, maids and chauffeurs. The Depression stole most of their accumulated wealth, and, as Nora put it, they were down to the occasional cleaning lady.

Nora's father graduated from Yale and MIT. As a child, Nora was taken to museums and concerts and art galleries, inculcated with the manners and appreciations of the upper-middle class. Her mother was determined to expose her children to "more than school and bread and butter," a philosophy Nora was determined to follow, even when she found herself a single parent with two kids, newly divorced. She had to find a job that would enable her to provide not just the basics but the extras for her children.

It occurs to me that you have to have had previous exposure or awareness of finer things in order to recognize their value to your children. In my family, manners were reduced to whatever would liberate you from the kitchen table without getting whacked, and the "finer things" involved Sunday drives and the occasional dinner at A & W. More like Roseanne's evil twin than "Dallas."

You also need a lot of self-esteem to confidently decide, "I will get a well-paying job without spending a minute thinking about being on social assistance." Education doesn't hurt, either. Fifty-eight out of sixty members of Nora's graduating class went on to university.

Born into what I think of as the "lost-out" generation, just pre–baby boom, Nora says there wasn't much questioning going on: you obeyed your parents and your teachers; middle-class values and expectations weren't suspect, everyone you knew bought into them. You provided your children with at least as much as you had, and that meant, for a divorced woman, getting a job. Nora's mother still works, at eighty-eight, bound and determined not to be a burden to her children. It's what a responsible person does, Nora believed. (She smiles at me across the table: "I'm much more thoughtful now than I was at thirty.")

"But it seems these days that most people who've managed

for themselves have resentments and difficulties empathizing with those who haven't had the same success. How have you avoided that trap?" I ask.

Neither of us is particularly fond of the feminist use of the word "privilege," but there are times when it's unavoidable.

"Poverty was masked in those days. Of course it existed, but it hadn't spilled out onto the streets. It helped me to work as a researcher for the *Toronto Star*, especially on pieces such as the one that delved into the living conditions of those on the 10,000-person waiting list to get into Ontario Housing. I knew that I'd been very lucky most of my life, that I hadn't been dealt a bad hand. I still feel that, even after Brennan's diagnosis."

In this age of victim one-upmanship, Nora could safely claim tragedy and hardship. When your son succumbs to voices suggesting he knock you off, when all his potential is ravaged by something called schizophrenia, self-pity might be in order.

"I don't want sympathy, I feel it's misplaced: it should, or empathy should, go to Brennan and others diagnosed with mental illness."

Instead, Nora has become a friend of the psychiatric survivor community, pushing for autonomy and dignity rather than locked wards and more medication.

She is one of those whose volunteer efforts, Mr. Harris assured taxpayers, would take on the roles previously played by government. She hates being part of band-aid solutions to real problems, hates it more that Harris will point to her and others like her and say, "See, it works."

She knows it doesn't work, knows the dangers of turning need into charity, but the alternative is simple: people will go hungry, people will freeze to death.

Like David Reville, she went through what she'd call a bad patch when, for a few years, she didn't have paid work. In spite of a lifestyle that is comfortable and not threatened, in spite of long hours on committees and boards dealing with mental health issues, in spite of extraordinary accomplishments, such as being an instrumental part of opening an "Out of the Cold" shelter at the Queen Street Mental Health Centre, she found her self-esteem assaulted and corroded by the "just a housewife" syndrome.

In the last few months, I've seen the change in her as she happily goes about her new work, writing for *Elm Street* magazine. Her confidence has increased markedly, she looks better, her self-assurance is evident. She agrees; other people have also remarked on the change.

It is distressing to realize once again the extraordinary impact of social expectations and stigma on the comfortable and strong, without the added effects of deprivation, want and hunger. But I shake off that thought and return to the subject that most preoccupies me. I have naively assumed that she can give me some formula, or some map that I can suggest people of good will follow in order to break through class barriers and assumptions. After all, *we're* friends.

Nora quickly disabuses me of that reassuring notion.

"I don't consider you to be 'a poor person.' It's just a difficult time for you right now."

It's true, on reflection, that I have been working through most of the time that I've known the Slingers. But I've never lost the sense of, for lack of a better term, "class roots" or "class loyalties." I've also been constantly aware, because of my debilitating bouts of depression, of the impermanence of salaried life, which is the hallmark of my existence. For me, poverty is what feels like the normal state, moneyed life the blip.

Nora doesn't agree with my societal divisions. She sees this as a stratified society rather than a class-restricted society. She's also disabusing me of my assumption that she's been able to bridge those class boundaries.

"I'm the only one?" I ask, shocked. Meaning, am I the only person of my class you know? I'm rapidly trying to figure out why I thought this wasn't the case.

"Except for your sister Dianne."

Recognizing that she's blown my premise, she calmly waits out my rethinking.

"You know, when I go to events like June's seventieth birthday party, or dinners at your house, or Joey's book launch at Jack Rabinovitch's," I say, "I look for people like me. I guess it's natural. But aside from the occasional Nellies' staff, or your daughter's friends, there's no one I feel safe with, or have anything in common with. And that's not class commonality, it's more generational, I guess. Look at your own circle, how many of your friends have friends who are out of their particular class?"

"But Pat, it's quite likely that many people have come from working-class families, but they've learned to adopt the camouflage: how to dress, how to talk, what to talk about."

"Yes, but they don't keep the attachments to that working class, it's usually an embarrassment best left behind."

Nora confesses:

"When I go into PARC, or the Queen Street Mental Health Centre, I feel the same degree of discomfort. And there's no camouflage I can adopt that will help me blend in, even if I dress down. I don't know how to start a conversation, what to talk about. I'm terrified I'll come across as a 'Lady Bountiful' type. I'm afraid of giving offence. It's different if you're doing something together, when I sit with survivor activists on committees, when we can talk politics."

It's much more than a problem of income, of course; life experience itself creates huge gulfs. I sometimes watch Nora and Joey together: it's so heartening to see how they support each other, take pride in each other—and it's so utterly foreign.

Their daughter Andrea displays an impressive level of social ease, and even Brennan networks with a skill and comfort level beyond me.

"But if there are no bridges between the classes, no opportunities for getting to know each other's lives better, what hope is there to end class war? You hear of groups of Palestinians and Israelis getting together, Irish Catholics and Protestants meeting, Croatians and Serbs—it's the only way to deal with prejudice, with hate, with the easy devaluing of another human being. God, I'm guilty of it myself, the assumptions I made about Reva Gerstein before I ever talked to her, about the lawyers and business leaders and bankers I've encountered on boards and committees."

I'm thinking of a bunch of things at once: Nora noticing the still-wet jeans hanging in my bathroom, realizing that I was hand-washing them, carefully suggesting that I make use of her washer and dryer.

As we emptied one machine, she started loading in Brennan's clothes, switching to hot water, squirting and squirting and squirting stain remover over socks and underwear, clearly despairing at the state of his clothes, which he seems to wear forever, at the state of his existence, represented so starkly by this small mound of laundry.

Nora, with casualness and flair, hosting a dinner for twenty-five people, keeping an eye on the comfort level of her guests.

Relaxing in the chaos of my room.

Joey sweltering, remarkably patient as he sits on the only chair in my room, showing me how to save my writing on disks.

I can ask them about the invisible rules that become visible only when you break them. If they say, "Come about seven," I can demand clarification: what does that really mean? I don't settle for, "Whenever you get here," I hold out for what's socially acceptable.

Nora still doesn't quite understand why my sister Dianne won't show up at parties, why events at her house would be viewed as intimidating. Even as she recognizes how long it took, as she puts it, for me to show "a comfort level." It's no longer a discomfort with her or Joey, although he can sometimes seem a little formidable, it's just that her circle is not one with which either of us has a natural trust.

Like other members of our class, we, when out of our element, are alive with sensitivities to judgments and putdowns and missteps—of us, of where we come from, of what we believe. It's difficult when you're judged by someone else's rules, most of which you don't even know, and are not afforded the dignity of being granted the measure of who you are, isolated from any other factor.

–.–.–

THE TORY REVOLUTION HAS
"PEOPLE LIKE US" ON A ROLL

... Before Harris, it was generally assumed in
Ontario that government had a role to play....

No more. Now the buzzwords inside government are "self-reliance" and "private sector"....

Harris has replaced the notion of the public
with that of the taxpayer....

For Harris, the term special interest is
reserved for those who are not "like us"—
union leaders, doctors, natives, social workers,
poor people, and teachers.

The key role of government is to reduce the
power of these others so that "people like us"
may flourish.

(Thomas Walkom, *Toronto Star*, June 8, 1996)

—.—.—.—

I know a man who adopted a child with Down Syndrome.
She's a teenager now, and when I met them together at a
downtown hotel I was struck with a few truths represented by
her beaming smile.

He never considered plastic surgery to alter the physical

features of her disability. Some parents do, supposedly for the good of the child. I realized, as we joked about how cool her dad was (and she believes he is very cool), what a mistake we make when we put a disabled child next to a "normal" child to judge issues like quality of life. Taken for who she is, all of who she is, this is a wonderful young woman, in and of herself. She has no need or time for pity.

That's the worst part of current governments, this refusal or inability to see the dignity, the striving, the heroism of those caught up in poverty. And that's also the worst part of class divisions—we make assumptions that become set in concrete, that reduce lives to the trappings of lives.

I know people who can spot an undercover policeman at fifty paces. It has less to do with shoes than teeth, bearing, eyes and attitude. When I search for affinities in a crowd of the well-to-do, I look less at outfits than at faces. (After all, as Nora reminds me, though I don't adopt camouflage per se, I also don't dress poor: more counter culture.) The results of long-term poverty are clear to see, almost impossible to hide. And in gatherings of the elite, this can lead to abrupt dismissals. The culture of poverty versus the culture of culture.

Nora's eyes always water after a few hours with me, her allergy to tobacco taking a severe beating. We've eaten supper and moved inside the café, the night air having chilled. I remind her of the telegram I sent to her and Joey some years back, after he'd written a piece about a dinner where I'd received the Canadian Mental Health Association's Hinks award. He'd used (knowing I loved it) a lot of cowboy imagery in the column, and I was quite touched. The telegram read in part: "You guys are either going to have to marry me or adopt me."

"I think you've decided to adopt me."

Nora grins back, remembering. She's been trying to persuade me to accept a key to their house, so I can come at any time to use their washer and dryer, their computer.

"And if you happen to want to stay for a while, who'd know?"

She is not motivated by charitable impulses; if she were I wouldn't have anything to do with her. She is, though few years separate us, very much a mother, and very much an open and generous spirit. Though we know there is a formula here, neither of us can read it.

She pays for our repast with one of a vast array of credit cards, and we go out onto the busy downtown street, two unlikely friends who beat the odds to come together.

 never felt like I was middle class. I didn't live in a renovated house, we didn't have cable or colour television, junk food, ketchup in bottles, new cars, yearly family vacations. My mother says: 'Of course you were raised in a middle-class family. You went to camp, you took gymnastics and ballet, you read books for entertainment, both your parents were educated and working.'

"But to me, it seemed that second-hand clothes and home cooking (we never went to restaurants) were less of a lifestyle choice than an economic necessity. This is not to say I felt I was poor. I got everything I needed, just not what I wanted. I was envious of my friends. While we only had two channels on a black-and-white TV, a huge treat was going to lunch at my girlfriend's. We'd eat hot dogs and watch 'The Flintstones.' It seemed at the time they had all the luxuries: Pop Tarts for breakfast, white bread, while at home I was crunching stale granola and wheat germ and watching my mother make ketchup out of tomatoes and molasses."

Although I am a friend of her parents, and almost twice her age, attitudinally we are more in sync than I would have suspected. Lisa is bright, funny, very attractive and exudes warmth.

"I would say I was raised with more hippie values than middle-class ones. But I do see what she means when we go to dinner with my aunt's family. Her grown-up sons are university educated, worldly, and after dinner everyone sits around reading books. I like books too, but I feel like, isn't there something else we could be doing? Something fun? Anyway, when I see them, I realize that I haven't turned out the way I was probably meant to. Here I am, barely a high school graduate, with a two-and-a-half-year-old child and a husband eleven years older than me. No career, no sophistication. I used to feel pretty intimidated around them, until I started feeling more comfortable with myself."

School was difficult for her. She understands it has to do with family stuff more than intelligence, her brother's short, troubled life impacting heavily on her own.

"I was wondering," I ask her, treading a bit carefully, "if you see him in the faces of the Squeegee Kids downtown?"

The Squeegee Kids have been the subject of some heated controversy, punks with strangely dyed and shaped hair who lunge at the windshields of cars stopped at traffic lights, more often smearing the glass than cleaning it and upsetting drivers who feel intimidated into "donating" spare change.

"Oh, absolutely. But at least they are doing something. My brother and his friends just panhandled."

It could be said he was ahead of his time: in his professed anarchy, his almost total alienation. He left home at fourteen.

"I was twelve, and I followed him out to the streets, to the apartment he shared with his friends. He didn't mind me hanging around, we were pretty close. And of course I was the go-between—my parents and him didn't talk much. I'd watch him panhandle for enough money to party on weekends, and it didn't seem degrading at all. He was my big brother, handsome and strong and tough. Everyone on the streets knew him, he was their hero. Their leader. It wasn't about who was the most together, it was about who was the craziest. He had the most tattoos, the most razor cuts, he screwed the most girls, drank and didn't fall down, did drugs and didn't crash. Of course, what it really was was that he could play-act the best, perform the best. I stopped thinking that bunch was cool after his suicide. He was fifteen. I never saw any of them again, partly because I needed to blame someone, partly because I didn't understand how they couldn't see—they lived with him—he was suffering."

It seemed like all the trouble with her brother had left her no room to be anything but the good child, at least while he lived.

At thirteen, she chose new friends and new behaviours.

"They weren't the middle-class kids I'd hung out with when I wasn't with my brother. They were kids who lived in housing projects like Regent Park, Donmount Court. Kids who spent late nights in clubs, dancing and drinking and smoking dope. I was the only one who had to lie about what I was doing—either their mothers were just too tired from working all day to try and enforce rules, or they were nurses doing night shifts. There didn't seem to be any fathers living at home."

Skipping school, sneaking out the basement window at night—none of this made learning any easier.

"I didn't feel very good about myself back then. I was getting in over my head. It's like, you skip one class, and you can't go to the next one, because how do you account for the one you missed? I quit in grade ten. Went out to work. Of course, the only work I could get were low-paying, service-oriented jobs that did nothing to make me feel better about who I was. I decided to go back, and my parents paid for an alternative school that I really liked. I graduated."

At the age of nineteen, she met her husband at a club. They exchanged phone numbers and were soon an item. He and his two partners had their own business they were trying to get off the ground at the time. They had a condo down at Harbourfront that served as both a ritzy address for their property management firm and their home. Because he was seen as the most financially credible, he signed the lease for the condo and for the necessary business equipment. Times got tough, his partners melted away, and he was left with the debts and obligations.

She pitched in, and between the two of them they managed to keep the fledgling business afloat for another year. When it finally collapsed, he went back to work as a collections officer at a large trust company, and she once again found herself doing the kind of jobs she'd done when she first left high school.

"I got pregnant. We'd wanted children, perhaps not at that very moment, but we were excited all the same. My mother was happy for me, because I'd always said I'd never have kids, so my attitude and approach to life had clearly improved in her eyes. I spent most of my time vomiting. Work was not a practical consideration."

The death of her grandmother led to an unexpected inheritance of $40,000 when she was twenty-three. Now the mother of a beautiful girl, it seemed to her sensible and adult to use that as a down payment on a house.

"It's about a hundred years old. A semi-detached, narrow building, with three small bedrooms. I don't feel like I own any of it really, except for a few of the kitchen tiles."

It wasn't easy getting a mortgage, even with 25 percent in cash to lay down. She confesses she wasn't entirely honest about her work history, but she couldn't figure out any other way to pull it off. At any rate, they got it, and moved in, with a premature sigh of relief.

Her husband puts in about nine hours a day, five days a week, bringing home $2,000 a month. Their mortgage payment, land tax, hydro and gas, house and life insurance come to $1,500 a month. At the best of times, there's not a lot to spread around.

There's a lot of tension, a lot of arguments about money.

"But I know—I just have to look around—how lucky we are. We're never hungry, there's always food to eat. We used to be able to pay all our bills. There wasn't anything for recreation, for new clothes, any extras really. But we're never hungry. And I have my parents, who are ready to babysit when they can."

For almost a year, they took in some friends who'd lost their housing, hoping that sharing their limited space would take some of the financial pressure off. But their friends could contribute very little, and it ended up costing more than it brought in.

Just after their friends managed to find a place of their own, she had a bad fall, breaking her ankle so badly surgery had to be done, and a metal pin inserted, to effect repairs.

There were cabs to pay for, to go back and forth to medical and physio appointments, parking fees when they had the use of her father's car, medication, babysitting, ordering in meals because she couldn't stand long enough to cook. They couldn't, for the first time in two years, make their mortgage payment.

"I felt totally intimidated. I knew I had to call the company, but I couldn't bring myself to do it. The house is in my name, because of the failure of my husband's business, so it was up to me to deal with whoever I had to deal with."

Her husband tried to both reassure and coach her. After all, collections was what he did.

"Most people, when they default on a payment, lay low, you know, hide. But companies aren't gung-ho about repossessing property, they're more interested in working things out, or at least they used to be. By calling and explaining what had happened, I would get points up front. I kept building up my courage, telling myself it's not like being called to the principal's office. I'm an adult.

"And whoever I would be speaking to would be a human being, just like me. And I knew how my husband handled people; he wasn't a threatener or a leg-breaker. He would often try to help his clients find jobs so that they could meet their obligations, try to work things out. Even to the point of lending them money out of his own pocket. He's decent. So finally I did it.

"The first person I talked to at the company seemed to be quite nice, even understanding. But the guy who called me back was very heavy, very intimidating. He left me no room to move, not even to breathe. 'This is a very serious situation. What are your intentions?' People came to the house, I pretended I wasn't home. All these heavy messages left on my answering machine. I know more than the average person about repossessions, about the law, but I was so scared. I could end up with virtually nothing.

"Clearly, they were getting a lot tougher a lot sooner than they did even a year ago.

"Finally we came to an agreement. That is, I agreed that we would pay, on top of the regular mortgage payment, an extra $500 in October and an extra $549 in November."

"If you only have $500 a month left over after your regular payment, how are you going to manage?"

Although she still needs a cane to get around and has been confined to her place long enough to go somewhat stir-crazy, she's taken in an eight-month-old infant whom she cares for from 8:30 to 5:30, every weekday, for $20 a day. She's also decided to advertise for a toddler. Now she is part of the underground economy.

If she went out to work, she'd have to pay for day-care for her daughter, now four years old, which would pretty well eat up whatever she earned. She soldiers on.

"I can't imagine trying to raise my child alone. I have

friends that are on social assistance, that can't afford, even on subsidy, to pay for the bus to take their child to day-care. Or pay for a phone. Their isolation, which I've had just a taste of as I've been confined to my house, is unimaginable. There's no support out there for them. I want my child to know her father. So we're pretty determined to make it work for us. In spite of the pressure, the tension. I mean, I'd never stay in a bad situation, but I'm going to make this work."

've gone off music. Instead, CNN plays eigh-
teen hours a day, as evocative as Tchaikovsky,
as otherworldly as a Faustian opera.

I watch one set of Irish men and women
surround another set of Irish men and
women, prepared to kill for the freedom to
march thigh-deep in the blood of history.

I watch Benjamin Netanyahu open disputed
land for the settlers who will have to be
eventually disarmed and forcibly evicted and no doubt charged
with the murder of their own leadership.

I despair of keeping track of the ethnic and tribal hatreds
in Rwanda and Burundi, or the body count in Chechnya.

Clinton signs the welfare bill, and still sleeps at night.

And in the last few days the great swell of discordance, the
New Age Wagnerian obscenity: Buchanan, Schlafly, North; the

Republican convention; the squeak and glittering ambition of Perot. I watch the faces of the cheering crowds, ordinary faces, vindicated faces, taxpayer faces. I hear the hooves of the Horsemen.

Surely the fat lady is singing. Harris's approval rating is still sky high. I heard a commentator say that Newt Gingrich won't use the word "revolution" any more to describe his activities in Congress; through focus groups he's learned that the electorate is more comfortable with the term "common sense."

-.-.-

NEW JERSEY'S GOVERNOR LAUDS HARRIS'S MOVES

America's version of Mike Harris came north with a simple message for the Ontario premier: keep up the good work. New Jersey Governor Christine Whitman, a Republican, passed through Toronto yesterday uttering phrases now familiar across Ontario: "common sense," "open for business," and "leaner and smarter." But she was referring to the politics of her own state, not this province.

Since becoming New Jersey's first female governor in November 1993, Whitman has cut personal income taxes by 30 percent, lowered taxes and reduced regulations on business, proposed privatizing government services ranging from day-care to motor vehicle registration and pushed for an easing in her state's labor legislation.

In response, Whitman's critics have accused her of throwing 3,400 low-paid public-sector workers on the street, forcing property taxes higher, reducing the health-care budget and chopping services to children, the disabled and the elderly.

And yes, [she] is well aware of similar criticism being leveled at Harris in Ontario for his pledge of a 30 percent personal income tax reduction, rollbacks of welfare rates, public-sector job cuts and scrapping of other government services and programs....

Harris didn't meet with Whitman yesterday, but just after she was elected—overcoming a large deficit in the polls by promising a 30 percent reduction in personal income tax—Harris met with her to talk about tax cuts and related issues.

"It's tough but you can get through it and it's worth it," Whitman said yesterday when asked about her latest advice to Harris. "If you really believe it's going to work, you stick with it."

(Daniel Girard, Toronto Star, July 28, 1995)

"DOLE IS A HARRIS WANNABE," SAYS GINGRICH

(Toronto Sun, October 28, 1996)

-.-.-

It's tough when the majority call for a lifeboat, ration supplies, determine who will stay afloat and who will be thrown over the side. That's the scary part, of course, of the kind of people who are in power right now: their brutal willingness to sacrifice other people. They don't know those other people, they certainly never socialize. It's easy to dismiss them as labels, as pathologies, as freeloaders when you haven't learned how to look at people, how to listen.

With the Harris government's approval rating still over 50 percent, it's become hugely important to me, even more so than usual, to hold on to my faith that reason and empathy might not have left the world. There are lengthy days when I feel like the old fellow with the lamp wandering through the streets of townships looking for an honest man—except I'd be using a disposable lighter and the search would be for a shrink-resistant soul.

I am in a perfect position to understand economic fears and

frustrations, but for the life of me I don't understand the willing handing over of the self to meanness, spite and ignorance. I do not believe it's a natural consequence of hard times, despite the evidence of history. People want to be better than that— until they're given licence by politicians and business leaders, until they can find their justification in media exposés on welfare rip-offs.

Few of those who share the kind of background, the diagnosis or the lifestyle that is mine get the same opportunities I do to converse with those in the middle to upper-middle classes. And, for that matter, few of those in the middle to upper-middle classes are exposed to someone like me. I've known since the heyday of the civil rights movement how important it is for people to actually talk to each other, to move beyond stereotypes towards commonalities. But where are the meeting places, where is the common ground?

It is clearer today than it's ever been that the majority of us will always help into power those who focus blame on others. Blame for life not being what we think it ought to be, blame for spiritual decay, blame for fears and failures and frustrations. Whether it be Jews or weaker countries or different ethnicities or the have-nots, the sense of other is sufficient to turn our sights away from what we have made of our lives and hate those who have robbed us.

I spent a lot of time in a lot of groups trying to get people to see each other as people. To relate to one another not as social worker to patient, not as psychiatrist to patient, but as people. Most of all, to learn to value what is good and decent about people, whatever their circumstances. It's sad that that's something we have to learn from and about people whose chief struggle, of all the struggles they have to fight, is for the right to contribute and to be seen as contributing members of the society that once rejected them.

It seems to me sometimes that we take a person in poverty, an individual suffering the misery of poverty, and we subdivide that misery into sections. Then we build huge support systems based on our assumptions about those stand-alone bits of misery:

welfare
children's aid
corrections
addictions
shelters
food banks
psychiatry
drop-ins

And while we successfully continue to employ all the helpers in the helping professions, and sometimes make great strides in treating one particular bit of misery, we continue to fail to see the individual and the source from which all the misery springs.

The operation is a success, but the patient dies.

—.—.—.—

HOMELESS TALE LOSES GRIT
No regular meetings, PM now says

Burnaby—Prime Minister Jean Chrétien now says he never actually meets regularly with a homeless man on the streets of Ottawa....

In his talk with students in Dauphin, Manitoba, Chrétien said he's learned from his conversations with the homeless that it's not always right for governments to step in to help the needy.

"There's one place I go to in Ottawa regularly and every day there is a man who is unfortunately and obviously sick. We just sit with a chair at the corner of the street," Chrétien said.

"But 20 years ago a person like that was in a hospital. Today we'll let them live in society.... He is better to have a form of freedom like that than to be in a hospital where he will be just a number."

Chrétien said sometimes there isn't much government can do for the homeless because they suffer from mental problems or drug abuse.

(Robert Fife, *Toronto Sun,* October 18, 1996)

The homeless, too, have learned to hallucinate someone to talk to. The poor, in all their manifestations (the elderly, the ill, the addicted, the down-sized), have got used to hearing the discussions and interpretations of their problems raging over their heads. We'll give grants to study the issues involved in homelessness, and hold inquests when some of them freeze to death in their freedom.

We haven't come to terms with any of this. One side talks about cutting, the other about keeping. Neither is interested in fundamental change.

For long years before Harris, before Newt and the push towards workfare, we realized in our community that the best possible cure for mental illness was work. People felt better when they had something positive to look forward to, when they stopped feeling acted on, treated, maintained, and started working in the system to change the system. To change perceptions.

At the moment, it seems the biggest costs of our social safety net are the salaries paid out to social workers, job counsellors, wel-fare workers and others, who tend to be children of the very same middle class who've expressed their anger at spiralling costs.

We have far too much invested in the status quo to return to basics: how people feel about themselves and their opportunities in life.

Many of the problems of the poor involve too many people receiving too much money to help the poor with their problems. Let the poor, the seniors and the disabled work with the poor, the seniors and the disabled. Stop the harmful and wrongheaded university training of social workers and case managers and professional advocates who, with the best intentions, continue to mine the consequences of poverty.

I didn't go to welfare, or to the Clarke Institute or vocational training or other "centres of excellence": I went to a tiny program, A-way Express, insignificant within the broader health budget, a program that employs psychiatric survivors, that is run by survivors: thirty people on welfare and disability, who are allowed to make $160 a month over their cheques. I was made welcome, I had people around me who understood what it feels like to be down and out, self-critical and nervous that learning new tasks will be an ordeal they can't overcome. There's a lot of laughter here, and much irreverence towards the rest of the system.

I was deeply touched that my community responded to my need without judgments, without accusations: they declared themselves proud to have me. People engaged in conspiracies of kindness: I was offered extra hours that other people turned down, because I was seen to need the income more. I kept hearing how I'd done so much for the survivor community, even while the survivor community was looking out for me.

It re-established my sense of myself as someone worthwhile, and that remains a constant, although my monetary worth still fluctuates wildly, as though on some dollar-value roulette wheel.

Depending on the day, the hour and the task, I can go from $7.50 a day as a courier to $300 a day as a consultant.

I don't know what waits for me.

The world has become a very cold place for those of us on the fringes of life.

‒.‒.‒

From the second-floor window of the A-way office, I watch a sad drama play itself out in the scrub of grass known locally as "Pigeon Park." There's usually an orderly routine to the activities of the people who use the space: early in the mornings, business men and women allow their dogs to play tag with the flocks of pigeons and gulls, tongues lolling, tails frenetically wagging, revelling in the moment the birds take to the air in small clouds. In the late afternoon, toddlers with their nannies in tow stumble, arms wide in wonderful embrace, into the bunched-up birds the way suburban kids race through puddles or piles of leaves.

The rest of the day, people whose lives or circumstances include neither children nor pets drop by, through some unwritten agreement, one at a time, preserving the specialness of the moment. With them they carry plastic bags of bread-crumbs to scatter to the eager, clamouring scavengers.

It's November, and the few trees in the park are barren, their skeletal branches emphasizing the bleakness of the season. Exactly one year, now, from the moment I counted up my resources and found I couldn't afford to live.

She is a regular, with her scarf and long coat and odd mannerisms. She sits in the same spot, every afternoon; the pigeons anticipate her arrival and start to gather around her bench minutes before she shows. Maybe it's just the affirmation of having little bits of life depending on her, expecting her. Maybe it's just something that breaks up the lonely tedium of the day. It's her moment, and she's usually left in peace to enjoy it.

Today, a boy about ten years old stands and watches from a safe distance as she settles on her bench and reaches into her bag to scatter the crumbs she's saved. Pigeons and gulls pile atop one another, squabbling, screeching, pecking aggressively in a frantic effort to feed. The boy darts into them, open-mouthed in what I assume is a yell, and they rise in alarm, retreating to the power lines parallelling the park. She is startled and looks towards where he stands now, triumphant and smirking. Reaching once again into her bag, shaking her head at the meanness of the child, she scatters her meagre bounty and the birds fly down to her, only to have the boy repeat his run and shout.

The woman and the boy, yards apart, stare at each other. She rises and walks towards him; he retreats a bit, then stands firm. I watch as she turns back, and this time, as carefully as if she were planting seeds, drops crumbs near the base of the tree nearest her bench, thinking perhaps that it will offer some protection against the willful child.

The birds stay watchful on the wires. She returns to her bench. The boy saunters to the tree, grinding the crumbs disdainfully and deliberately under his feet, while she stands abruptly in disbelief and shock. Near her bench, two men sit in conversation, and she approaches them, arms held out in supplication. She is clearly appealing to them; they shrug her away and continue talking.

She stands in confusion for a moment, then tries to appeal

to the drivers of idling cars parked on the side street, gesturing to the boy, who is clearly realizing that no one will intervene.

The phone rings, pulling me away, and I spend minutes taking orders, impatient and distressed that I can't leave my office and fix things for her. When I can get back to my window, the woman is gone, and the boy is perched precisely in her spot on her bench, enjoying his victory.

There's a lovely piece of graffiti on a building in my neighbourhood: "It's the day after the end of the world."

Most of the time, I feel like that, like a very important part of people has died. But there are moments of light and joy, such as when the trees and their stark branches are decorated with—it seems at times—hundreds of sparrows and starlings singing to the close of day. And the promise of tomorrow.

I go on.